D0261739

TREFOREST SHORT LOA

1. The lo

Comedia Series ● No 11

What's this Channel Four?

An alternative report

Edited by Simon Blanchard and David Morley

Comedia Publishing Group
9 Poland Street, London W1V 3DG   Tel: 01-439 2059

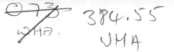

Comedia Publishing Group (formerly Minority Press Group) was set up to investigate and monitor the radical and altenative media in Britain and abroad today. The aim of the project is to provide basic information, investigate problem areas, and to share the experiences of those working within the radical media and to encourage debate about its future development. For a list of other titles in the series see page 187/188.

First published in 1982 by Comedia Publishing Group
9 Poland Street, London W1V 3DG. Tel: 01-439 2059

© In all editorial matter Comedia Publishing Group and the editors.

© All contributions copyright the authors.

ISBN 0 906890 28 4 (paperback); ISBN 0 906890 29 2 (hardback)

Comedia especially wishes to thank the Channel Four Users' Group for their financial contribution to the production of this publication.
We would like to thank The Guardian for permission to reprint the article by Richard Bourne, and City Limits for permission to reprint the articles by Youth Television and by Sue Clayton.

For helping to make this book possible, thanks to: Crispin Aubrey, Helen Baehr, Rob Burkitt, Cinema Action, the Channel Four Users' Group, Mike Elliott, Simon Hartog, Chris Hird, the Independent Film-makers Association, Local Radio Workshop, Roger Shannon, Dafydd Elis Thomas, Phillip Whitehead.

Designed by Pat Kahn
Illustrations by Will Hill
Diagrams drawn by Sandra Oakins

Photographs by Angharad Tomos/Welsh Language Society; Channel Four Television. 'Life or Death' pamphlet cover courtesy of Plaid Cymru.

Typeset by Red Lion Setters
22 Brownlow Mews, London WC1

Printed in Great Britain by
Unwin Brothers Limited, The Gresham Press, Old Woking, Surrey

Trade Distribution by
Marion Boyars, 18 Brewer St, London N1

Introduction

Several motives prompted the putting together of this Alternative Report. Firstly, the arrival of Channel Four TV Company Ltd. and the Welsh Fourth Channel Authority are both events of great importance, not only for broadcasting but for social life and politics more generally. They deserve informed discussion and analysis. Which brings us to the second motive. Under the terms of Sections 43 and 52 (2) of the Broadcasting Act 1981 the Independent Broadcasting Authority and the Welsh Fourth Channel Authority are required in their respective Annual Reports to show how they have carried out the duties laid on them by Parliament, namely, to ensure that Channel Four is 'distinctive'; and to provide a high quality fourth service in Welsh.

This raises two problems. Firstly, the idea that Parliament will watch over the broadcasters in any regular and systematic way is, as Phillip Whitehead has put it, 'in general, pretty much of a joke. The broadcasting Vote is not debated. Such debates as there are on broadcasting are not well attended . . . most Members choose to stay at home and watch the television.' Secondly, this absence of detailed scrutiny has allowed the IBA to become judge in its own cause; its Annual Reports are minor masterpieces in the art of self-esteem, containing little genuinely new information and even less analysis. In the private world of the Authority and the ITV and ILR companies everything is, if not quite perfect, then nearly so. (Though of course, there *is* room for improvement etc etc). As Sir Robert Fraser – the Authority's Director General in the late 60s – put it, catching the companies out has been considered 'at best childish and at worst a bore'.

In recent years these attitudes have become more pronounced, reaching an all-time low in the decision to appoint John Whitney (Managing Director of Capital Radio) as the IBA's next Director General. The mediocrity of Capital Radio's broadcast output is now a matter of record,[1] yet it would be pointless to blame the management of Capital, or those who own it, for the performance of this juke-box 'with a human face'. Responsibility for making each contractor's performance at least equal their promises rests with the IBA, and the failure to assert adequate control is theirs, not that of the private business operations which constitute commercial broadcasting. To invite Mr Whitney to take up the IBA's most senior executive post is entirely in keeping with the Authority's deep-rooted misunderstanding of who it should be ultimately responsive and responsible to.

We felt it best to start with some of the historical background to the emergence of the two Fourth Channel organisations. For it is only by understanding how they are an attempt to resolve a contradictory set of pressures that we can begin to make sense of the decisions finally taken. To uncover the meaning of the 'solutions' arrived at we need to investigate the problems that were being 'solved'.

All too quickly the two organisations will acquire a distinct character – a set of routines and traditions which can be taken for granted as obvious, natural, the 'right' way to do things. We have tried to make use of the time before they go on air to begin asking questions about what they have done so far, and what this may imply for their future performance.

The questions asked in each section of the book do not all spring from the same set of assumptions, nor do they arrive at identical conclusions. We do not see this as a disadvantage. Our aim has been to open up a debate, not close it down.

Nonetheless there is one central issue to which many of the contributions here address themselves. Who are the 'British' in British Broadcasting? Does 'British' effectively mean *English* (cf. Tomos, Coe)? does it mean *white* (cf. Sakaana)? does it mean *male* (cf. Hilton, Women's Advisory and Referral Service Action Group)? does it mean *over 30* (cf. Youth TV)? This is to raise a set of questions about the manner in which broadcasters address their audiences and the kinds of assumptions that they make about those audiences – questions to which both Channel Four and the Welsh Fourth Channel Authority will have to address themselves.

Changing institutions

Arguments over the control, finances and character of a fourth TV service go back more than 20 years – to the early days of commercial TV. The two-part account below is intended as a short and very basic outline for understanding how and why the Fourth Channel Company which goes on the air in November in England, Scotland and Northern Ireland came to be organised in the ways described: as a wholly owned subsidiary of the Independent Broadcasting Authority, funded by subscriptions from the ITV companies, and required by law to be, in a number of ways, 'distinctive'.

It is by intention a highly selective account, one which concentrates on the major shifts in broadcasting policy which provided the conditions for the start of a fourth service. The debates and decisions sketched in part I are only some of the pressures that affect how Channel Four will operate. Part II lays out the main financial, programming and scheduling mechanisms by which the company will be steered. In which directions they will take it remains to be seen. Those who would like to follow the arguments in more detail will find a selection of the published sources, such as they are, listed in the footnotes.

Where do new channels come from?

Simon Blanchard

PART I   DEBATES: THE FOURTH CHANNELS
WE MIGHT HAVE HAD

The BBC launched the world's first public TV service from Alexandra Palace in November 1936, a service abruptly shut down on the outbreak of war. Restarted in June 1946, when viewers were required to take out a 'combined sound and TV' licence, it had an audience nine months later of less than 15,000. But by 1951 there were nearly 600,000 viewers, by 1956 the total had reached 6 million and by the middle of 1960s virtually every home in Britain had a television set.

In 1949 the Labour government set up a Committee of Inquiry, chaired by Lord Beveridge, to consider the future of broadcasting. This Committee issued its report in January 1951, and its central recommendation was that the BBC should retain its monopoly position in providing broadcasting services.[1] This was the view of all the members of the Committee except one – Selwyn Lloyd – who wrote a dissenting Minority Report arguing that the BBC's monopoly should be broken up, and space for (controlled) commercial broadcasting made available.[2]

In the event, it was the perspective outlined by Selwyn Lloyd which prevailed. As a result of a vigorous campaign orchestrated by advertisers, some Tory MPs, TV set manufacturers and others, the Conservative government under Winston Churchill was talked into passing the 1954 Television Act. This authorised the establishment of the Independent Television Authority (ITA), and led in turn to the start of the London ITV service (provided by Associated TV at weekends and Associated Rediffusion on weekdays), which began broadcasting in September 1955. This was the start of advertising-financed TV programmes, and the other regional ITV companies followed soon after.[3]

The decision to allow the BBC to provide a second, complementary TV service (BBC-2) was the end point of a further round of discussions about the development of the broadcasting system. In the summer of 1960 the Conservative government set up another Committee of Inquiry, chaired by Sir Harry Pilkington, to review the state of broadcasting since the arrival of competition, and to consider – among other matters – who should provide a third TV service, and when. The Committee published its Report in June 1962,[4] and its two key findings were:

1. That 'the service of independent television does not successfully realise the purposes of broadcasting as defined in the Television Act,' a failure said to be the result of an 'organic weakness' in the relationship between the ITA and the ITV companies.
2. That 'the next TV programme should be provided by the BBC' and that this should be authorised 'as soon as possible.'

As a consequence of its criticisms the Report also proposed a number of changes in the constitution and organisation of the ITA/ITV systems. However, in its examination of the question of frequency allocation the Committee did agree that it was technically feasible to provide in the longer term for up to six TV networks. It therefore offset its criticisms of the existing ITA/ITV structure by stating that 'if, after independent television as reconstituted and re-organised has had sufficient time to adapt itself to its new constitution, it has proved its capacity to realise the purpose of broadcasting, it should be authorised to provide a second programme. We hope that it will be possible to authorise this within five years of the reconstitution'.[6] With this remark, the (conditional) possibility of a fourth channel was clearly written on to the broadcasting agenda.

As it turned out, the Conservative government gave its attention, in passing the 1963 Television Act, to altering the basis for taxation of the independent TV contractors, and the Post Master General Reginald Bevins did no more than make a few polite noises about the possibility of a second commercial channel.[7] BBC-2 got off to what proved to be a very shaky start (in April 1964), and in October of the same year the Labour Party, under its new leader Harold Wilson, scraped home to victory in the General Election with a working majority of just four.[8]

The debate gets shelved

At first the Labour government was concerned, above all, after 13 years out of office, to hang on to its tiny majority and to pick a suitable moment to try and increase it – which it did successfully in the General Election of March 1966. In any case, as Richard

Crossman's diaries show, its energies were fully occupied in the broadcasting arena in working out what to do about pirate radio and the finances of the BBC.[9] Any possibility of a lively discussion about a fourth TV service was eventually knocked firmly on the head when Labour finally published its Broadcasting White Paper in December 1966. This said: 'However it were allocated, a fourth television service would make large demands on resources. The three main services of television already provide a large volume of programmes of various kinds and the Government do not consider that another television service can be afforded a high place in the order of national priorities . . . The Government have decided that no allocation of frequencies to a fourth television service will be authorised for the next three years at any rate.'[10]

It would have been reasonable to expect that, even if no-one else did, the ITV companies would kick up a fuss. But they were not well placed to do so. For shortly afterwards the ITA made its first announcement about the impending re-advertisement of ITV franchises, and to the dismay of many of the existing contractors, decided to make substantial changes in the transmission areas and scheduling pattern.[11]

The interesting tale of winners and losers in what *The Guardian* called 'the great 1967 tele-rush' is not of direct concern here.[12] Nonetheless, one of its results – the inevitable organisational upheaval in ITV – was partly responsible for the financial and administrative instability that accompanied the contract pattern when the new companies began broadcasting at the end of July 1968. For the first time since the 1950s revenues had begun to fall; there was a spate of sackings and resignations, particularly at London Weekend TV (LWT), and a vigorous lobby began to develop for the removal of the levy on advertising revenue.[13] Under pressure, the government announced that it was referring the matter to its Prices and Incomes Board (PIB).

The PIB's Report, published in October 1970, turned out to be a mixed blessing for the contractors. Although it went some way towards meeting the companies' demands with its recommendation that the levy should be reduced (the net effect of which was a £6½ million addition to ITV earnings), this was linked in the findings to an assessment that ' . . . the financial outcome (is) . . . too problematical for us to recommend the opening of a second commercial service.'[14]

Despite the negative conclusions of the PIB, it was from the summer of 1970 until early 1972 that the first substantial phase of debate on the future of a fourth service took place. During this time two coalitions of interest took shape in opposition to each other.

On the one hand, the ITA and the 'Big Five' ITV companies had canvassed opinion and support from inside their sector for a submission to the Minister of Posts and Telecommunications, Christopher Chataway. Published in December 1971 and entitled '*ITV 2*', its main arguments were: 1. The service should be provided by the ITA and should – like BBC-1 and BBC-2 – be complementary and not competitive with the existing ITV service. 2. There should be no new programme companies appointed as a result of the needs of the new service. 3. The service should be national and take programmes from all sources, including the ITV regional companies and outside producing sources. 4. Transmission should begin in 1974 or, failing that, in 1976, when the new programme contractors had been decided.[15]

But against this, three main interest groups were opposed to the plans for an ITV-2. These were the TV4 Campaign, the Association of Broadcasting Staffs (ABS), the BBC staff union and the Association of Cinematograph, Television and Allied Technicians (ACTT), the main ITV technicians' union, all of whom shared a concern that the future direction of broadcasting policy was not getting the wide-ranging public discussion it clearly needed.

Dissatisfaction with the broadcasting services (both BBC and ITV) had risen rapidly in the 1960s[16] and was now widespread amongst both those working inside broadcasting and many sections of the audience. But two more specific justifications added to this feeling that the arguments were being muffled. Firstly, the previous Labour government had announced an inquiry into broadcasting policy (under the direction of Noel Annan, Provost of University College) shortly before the General Election. Christopher Chataway had moved promptly to shut this down. Secondly, a letter written by Brian Young (Director General of the ITA) in June 1971, and circulated widely within the ITV system, had concluded ominously that 'the present intention is not to have a public debate, but rather to make sure that anyone within ITV who wants to do so has a chance to join in the collective discussion.'[17] So if the over-riding aim of all the groups was to prevent this attempt to stifle debate, what were they individually arguing for?

The TV4 campaign

Formed publicly in November 1971, this was a loose coalition of 'people concerned about the future of British broadcasting'. It included media critics, journalists, disaffected TV producers, MPs, trade unionists, media pressure groups and advertising executives.[18]

In a memorandum *'Opportunities for the fourth channel'*, published in December 1971, the campaign expressed great scepticism about the ITA's plans, pointed to the widespread hostility towards an ITV 2 (a hostility which even extended to some of the smaller regional ITV companies[19]), and put forward a series of alternative uses and structures for the fourth service: educational, community based, experimental.

The range of interests under the TV4 Campaign banner were culturally and politically diverse, and therefore not easily reconcilable. Even so, they were all agreed on a set of minimum objectives – summarised in a motion put before the House of Commons on the December 2, 1971:

This House believes that a public inquiry into the structure and future of television broadcasting should be established as soon as possible; that the remaining television frequencies should not be allocated until such a public inquiry is held; and that the fourth television channel should not be allocated to the present independent television contractors.[20]

The Association of Broadcasting Staffs

As well as supporting the widely voiced need for a comprehensive review of broadcasting policy, the ABS put forward a more specific and distinctive proposal, outlined in a letter to Christopher Chataway in December 1971.[21] This suggested that the fourth service should take the form of a National Television Foundation (NFT), financially and editorially independent of the two existing systems. The letter said that the proposal was '...a realistic and superior alternative to the plan put forward by the Authority, which would do no more than split British television into two equal and comparable halves, each the mirror image of the other, with no new cultural concept to inspire them.'

In a subsequent letter to *The Times* in January 1972 Tom Rhys, the ABS President, described the NTF as '...the new type of impresario which British television needs. The Foundation would be free to collect money from any acceptable source, including learned institutions, research and cultural foundations, local and national authorities, public utilities and commercial organisations either for making programmes on their behalf or, under the Foundation's editorial control, transmitting programmes openly sponsored by the body paying for the privilege. The Foundation could also acquire income from overseas sales of its programmes, from publications prepared in book and cassette form in co-operation with established publishing houses, and from transmission of ITV and BBC productions which these organisations can find little opportunity of repeating or sometimes of showing at all.'[22]

The ACTT

Any proposals for change in the structure of broadcasting were a matter of great concern to the ACTT and it set up its own TV Commission to consider the issues. The Commission published its findings as *TV4: A Report on the Allocation of the Fourth Channel* in November 1971. This 53-page study set out the historical background, looked closely at the ITV-2 proposals and some of the alternatives, and included a number of appendices of key documents.[23]

ACTT's main conclusion was to support the need for a proper enquiry, stressing that 'it is a matter of basic commonsense for workers to demand a full analysis of all the alternatives before the structure of their industry is altered in any substantial way'. The union considered that the financial basis of ITV-2 'looks extremely weak. We should need to see more detailed financial estimates from the companies to convince us that the PIB was wrong to reject a second commercial channel on financial grounds'. Finally, it concluded that the introduction of ITV-2 as currently proposed would destabilise an already high risk industry, producing harmful effects on programme standards and pre-empting the other options for a fourth service which had not yet been fully developed or publicly examined.

Faced with this highly visible range of different opinions over 'ITV-2' and its alternatives, Christopher Chataway did not have the option of remaining quiet and hoping the issues would go away – the pressure was now on him to make the government's position clear. But Chataway was already heavily committed on the broadcasting front as a result of his very important decision – announced in March 1971 – to give the ITA responsibility for the development of a system of commercial local radio.[24] So in January 1972 he simply announced that the Conservatives were postponing any decision on the allocation of a fourth service. That this left matters unresolved was at least a negative victory for those wanting a proper debate, but it didn't deter the Independent Broadcasting Authority – the ITA's new name after July 1972 when it formally took responsibility for commercial radio – from submitting further plans for 'ITV-2' in July 1973.

The Annan Committee revived

When a Labour government returned to power in March 1974, it made two important decisions on broadcasting. Firstly, the Home Office now became the sponsoring department for broadcasting policy, and secondly, the new Home Secretary Roy Jenkins announced a revived Committee 'to consider the future of the broadcasting services'. This was to be chaired – as planned in 1970 – by Noel Annan, and it was asked to report in 2½ years.[25]

The Committee's Report, as finally published in March 1977,[26] was a massive volume, the product of some 1,500 submissions and working papers, 44 meetings of the full Committee and extensive discussion of the issues in the media. Its broad terms of reference required the Committee to give a lot of attention to issues other than a fourth TV service, but the discussion here is confined to the conclusions reached in Chapter 15, entitled 'The Open Broadcasting Authority'.[27]

The OBA was the Committee's solution to the question of how to allocate a fourth channel. After reviewing the arguments for an ITV-2 and those which – opposed to an ITV-2 – called for the Channel to be given over to educational, community or regional needs, the Report said that ' ... there was one other set of proposals which became for us steadily more attractive, because they went to the heart of the organisation of broadcasting.' This was the 'comprehensive scheme' proposed to the Committee by Anthony Smith for a National TV Foundation.

Smith, ex-editor of '24 Hours', member of the TV4 Campaign, and writer/researcher on broadcasting policy (including for the Annan Committee itself[28]), had been closely involved with the elaboration of the NTF idea, and in December 1974 he presented the Committee with a paper summarising the scheme and the arguments for it.[29] Arguing, as the ABS had done, that ' ... if the fourth channel is placed in the hands of the IBA and the companies it will complete the symmetrical straitjacket of broadcasting in Britain', he stressed that 'the most important single thing we should ensure ... is that the channel is placed outside the existing competitive strategy, outside the BBC/IBA duopoly ... Better not to award it at all than to place it in these particular wrong hands.' Instead, he suggested: 'What has to be achieved is a form of institutional control wedded to a different doctrine from existing broadcasting authorities, to a doctrine of *openness* rather than to balance, to expression rather than to neutralisation.' (emphasis added) The Committee stated its conviction that 'this is the right approach to the fourth channel,' and simply changed a Foundation into an Authority.

Drawing heavily on the themes of Anthony Smith's paper, the Committee described the OBA in the following terms: 'We do not consider that the OBA should be required to schedule a balanced evening's viewing in which sport, light entertainment, education, news, current affairs and all the other types of programmes are shown . . . The OBA should operate as a publisher and its obligations should be limited to those placed upon any other publisher . . . to see to it that its programmes were not libellous, did not incite crime, disorder, or racial hatred and were not obscene. Like any other Authority, the OBA would have to see that an overall balance was achieved in its programmes over a period of time, but we should like to see this done in new and less interventionist ways . . . In general, we recommend that the Authority should have the maximum freedom which Parliament is prepared to allow.'

Programmes broadcast by the OBA would fall into three broad categories: educational, those made by individual ITV companies including ITN, and, most importantly, 'programmes from a variety of independent producers. We attach particular importance to this third category as a force for diversity and new ideas.' In organisational terms, the Committee saw no need for the OBA itself to become involved in production, though it would need a continuity studio. And on the question of funding, the Committee outlined a range of sources very similar to those suggested by the ABS: sponsorship, block advertising,[30] charities and special interest groups, the Arts Council and the Open University, subscriptions, and – if needed – direct government grant. They recommended that the OBA should sell the advertising time itself. These recommendations were a considerable victory for those opposed to any sort of ITV-2, and were heavily influenced by the carefully timed interventions within the Committee of Labour MP Phillip Whitehead.[31]

One final aspect of the recommendations must be mentioned. The Report had been prepared at a time when the problems of inflation, general economic performance and government concern over public spending had reached a new level of intensity, culminating in what *The Sunday Times* later called 'The Day The £ Nearly Died'[32] and the subsequent I.M.F. loan. A number of submissions to the Committee had suggested that a fourth service was beyond national resources.[33] In sharp contrast with the vitality and optimism of its substantive proposals the Report said: 'We ourselves felt that in the present economic climate there was little possibility of any Government agreeing to allocate the channel in the immediate future . . . We therefore recommend that the fourth channel should not be allocated until the nation's economy will permit the kind of service we have outlined. This may not be until the 1980s.'

Responses to the OBA plan

With the Report published and a formal government response expected in due course, a wide-ranging debate developed on the Committee's findings. The range of views expressed, and the particular strengths and weaknesses of each of them, cannot be presented in detail here.[34] But two opposing standpoints can be identified.

Opposition to an Open Broadcasting Authority came most notably from the IBA, the ITV companies and from the ACTT. Central to their case was the view that the proposed financial base of the OBA was not realistic. Block advertising was unlikely to work, the other funding sources were insignificant, and the channel would have to rely on spot advertising and/or direct public subsidy. To base the OBA's fortunes on advertising, the income base of ITV, was in conflict with Annan's recommendation that separate broadcasting authorities should not compete for the same revenue source; if the money came direct from government the channel's independence was threatened. Moreover, the OBA's planning of a separate rather than complementary schedule would aggravate the damage to ITV revenues and threaten job security.

Instead, they recommended that the IBA should control the fourth service. This would be based on spot advertising sold by the existing ITV companies. By constructing a complementary schedule to ITV in which target quotas of 'new things in new ways' (the IBA suggested 15% independent production, 10-15% educational material, 10-15% from the smaller ITV companies) were placed, some at peak time, the service would not make major inroads into ITV or BBC audiences. These obligations could be included in the necessary legislation. However, they did not consider it appropriate to relieve a fourth service of the obligation to achieve a 'proper balance' in its programmes.

Finally, since such a service was financially workable, the decision to set it in motion could be taken straight away. In any case, since the Annan Report had proposed that the IBA would be responsible for the engineering and transmission of the OBA's output, work on the installation of the necessary new transmitters could and should begin as soon as possible, without prejudice to the government's decision on how the fourth service should be run.

The OBA supporters – for the most part those who had argued its case with the Annan Committee – were not convinced by these objections. In their view they failed to address the widely articulated need to open up the existing duopoly of employment and programme ideas. For them, the fourth service could provide a genuine extension of opportunities to innovate in broadcasting: that this involved some risk was not a danger but a challenge, one that had to be met if television was to evolve rather than stagnate.

On the question of finance they pointed out that, since the initial costs to the ITV companies of financing an ITV-2 before it generated any income would undoubtedly be offset against their TV Levy payments, the public (through lost revenue to the Exchequer) would be the ultimate funder in any case. They also took the view that an ITV-2's economic prospects had not been properly explored and therefore this financial support could become indefinite. With these points in mind, there was no good reason why the more imaginative concept of an OBA should not merit public funding. A mechanism to ensure the OBA's independence could be arrived at if the political will was present. It could not be a general audience competitor to ITV and the BBC channels since its legislative obligations would, of necessity, be very different and its programming strategy would have to reflect these duties.

These different views on the validity of an OBA were not, however, the only ones that mattered. In the autumn of 1977 the Home Office, under the supervision of Merlyn Rees and Lord Harris,[35] prepared a draft of the government's White Paper which would set out its response to the Committee's Report. This rejected all the Annan reforms as impractical, unnecessary or too expensive,[36] and proposed a Cabinet Committee to examine the draft in detail.[37] Its proposed members included no ministers known to take an interest in broadcasting policy and carefully *excluded* three ministers known to be in favour of reform: Tony Benn, Roy Hattersley, and William Rodgers.

Unfortunately for the Home Office, the then Prime Minister James Callaghan was, on this issue if not others, something like a radical. He threw out the draft White Paper and the proposed Cabinet Committee list. Putting himself in the chair and bringing in Hattersley, Rodgers and Benn he stacked the Committee in the opposite direction. And when the Committee met during the spring of 1978 it was lobbied vigorously by OBA supporters to the point where the reformers won most of the arguments. This reforming view was endorsed by the full Cabinet in mid-July, and the White Paper on Broadcasting was finally published on July 26, 1978.[38]

The version of the OBA offered in the White Paper provided few surprises. It was to give priority to '(a) educational programmes; (b) programmes catering particularly for tastes and interests which are not adequately catered for on the existing three services; and (c) programmes produced outside the existing broadcasting organisations.' It would not make programmes itself but instead commission, purchase or otherwise acquire them, and would be responsible for making arrangements for the sale of advertising. The IBA would be responsible for engineering and transmission. The White Paper accepted that 'in order to have an assured financial base, a minority channel of the kind envisaged is bound to need a measure of financial assistance from the Government, at any rate in the early years...' Nonetheless, it stressed that 'the Government will expect the OBA to look to advertising revenues of various kinds to provide, directly or indirectly, an important and increasing source of finance.' The White Paper was distinctly cautious about the revenues to be found in sponsorship or block advertising, and declared its intention to allow the OBA to carry spot adverts. It also noted that 'the OBA may wish to consider with the IBA the possibility of some complementary scheduling between the ITV channel and the fourth channel...'.

On the question of the obligations to be laid on the OBA the White Paper – as others had done – disagreed with the Annan Committee's recommendations. The OBA was to be bound, like the BBC and the IBA, by the requirements of due impartiality in matters of controversy, and would have to ensure that nothing broadcast incited crime or was offensive to public feeling.[39] It was however accepted that – since the OBA had a special obligation to seek out programmes which catered for minority tastes and interests – it would be inconsistent to require it to secure the usual 'proper balance' in the subject matter of its broadcasts.

The introduction to the White Paper expressed a commitment by the Labour government to bring in legislation for an OBA 'at the earliest opportunity'. No such early opportunity was found. The Home Office – unconvinced to begin with – spent the remaining months of the Callaghan government firstly in pursuing its case against 'open-ness' through the 'ABC' trial and the obstruction of Clement Freud's Freedom of Information Bill[40] and secondly, taking a central role in the 'civil contingencies' against strikes by public sector workers over low pay that dominated the winter months of 1978/79.[41] The government itself gradually tottered to defeat in the general election of May, 1979.

The Tory version

With a majority of 44 seats over all the opposition parties,[42] the new Conservative government made an immediate commitment on the fourth channel. In the Queen's Speech on May 15 it was announced that legislation would be introduced to place the fourth service under the IBA, subject to what were called 'strict safeguards'. In anticipation of more detailed statements from the Home Office and the IBA as to just what these safeguards would be, the various interest groups began once more to make their views known and, where necessary, revise them.

At its annual conference on 19-20 May the ACTT passed an emergency motion which read: 'This Conference, noting the newly-elected Government's promise of a Fourth Channel governed by the IBA, commits itself to urgent and effective action that will both safeguard the jobs of those currently working in ITV and create more employment opportunities for members in the laboratories, film production, educational technology and freelance areas. Conference urges the creation of a new organisation under the IBA, which would operate the Fourth Channel and would draw the majority of its programmes from a variety of British independent production sources other than the existing ITCA companies.[43] This perspective was endorsed at a further One Day Conference in July, and led to the setting up of a special committee to pursue the policy.[44]

At the Edinburgh TV Festival in September, two other specific sets of proposals and critiques were offered – from the Channel Four Group and the Independent Film Makers Association (IFA). The Channel Four Group, a cultural descendant of the TV4 Campaign, had emerged in the aftermath of the Annan Report to push for an independent fourth service, and had been involved in the lobbying over the Labour 1978 White Paper. It contained, in its own words, 'film and TV professionals working for both the BBC and ITV as well as independents and individuals concerned with broadcasting in academic and public life'. In their position paper for the Festival, *TV4: the case for independence*, the Group reiterated the need for a channel that was different in structure and aims to the existing three. They called for TV4 (*not* 'ITV-2') to be politically culturally and economically free of dominant ITV influence',[45] and made a number of legislative suggestions to ensure this:

1. TV4 to be run by a Board, under the IBA, responsible for the Channel's policy.
2. The Board to appoint a Programme Controller who would have responsibility for all decisions on commissioning, purchasing and scheduling of programmes.
3. There should be no obligation on the Controller to commit specific quotas of broadcast hours to present or future ITV contractors or their subsidiaries.
4. The Controller should be instructed by the Board to consider proposals for programme production and purchase from all available sources in the UK so as to encourage

diversity and ensure that at least 50% of its programmes came from sources having no direct or indirect association with an ITV company.

5. TV4 funding to come from advertising revenue, collected by an agency supervised by the IBA. The channel's initial costs to be drawn by the IBA from a levy on the ITV companies.

6. There should be no contractual commitment or assumption that the Channel's scheduling should be complementary to programming on other channels.

The IFA had been set up in 1974 to act as a forum and voice for those working outside, and often against, the mainstream of the commercial film industry. Its members included film-makers, distributors, exhibitors, critics and teachers.[46] As well as taking an active part in the discussions in the Channel Four Group, the IFA produced its own pamphlet for the Festival, *Channel 4 and Independence*.[47] This emphasised the position of broadcasting as a social and cultural sphere, and laid particular stress on the necessity to consider the aspirations of the television audience: 'Viewers tend to be the one interest group with no voice in debates over the future of the TV they will watch and, in the last analysis, pay for. One of the main aims of TV4 must be to lessen the gulf between the professional communicators (including ourselves) and the public we observe, question and on whose behalf we speak. The public must not be seen as a statistical aggregate of abstract individuals but as a complex body of diverse and distinctive people, with a whole hitherto unexplored range of potentialities, desires and concerns, and an interest in broadcasting beyond having their receptive attention sold by one third party to another. The audience – or rather audiences – should be enfranchised.'

The Association proposed a number of ways to achieve this: 'The role of the ITCA companies should be kept to a minimum', 'new types of co-operation between programme-makers and the people they are making programmes with or about should be encouraged'; there should be 'a determination to welcome the controversial, the committed and the unfamiliar.' Minority interest should mean more than minority leisure pursuit or passtime'; Scheduling should not simply be "complementary" to other channels but should also be challenging and implicitly and, on occasion, explicitly critical'; experimental workshops should be set up, and it should not 'be compulsory to make programmes with rapid pace, instant recognisability and conventional standards of image quality'; creative work with technicians and technologies 'should not be limited to "special effects" or special segments in, say, music programmes, but should be encouraged across the whole spectrum of TV'; in other words 'new ideas are going to demand innovation in the look and form of programmes'. These objectives, in the IFA's view, could only be secured if institutional safeguards were found to counter-balance the power and pressure of the market and the ITV companies. They therefore proposed that the IBA should set aside a proportion of revenue from TV4 to go to a Foundation charged with providing programmes of cultural and social value.

There is one other statement of position at the Festival which deserves mention, and one which attracted rather more publicity. This was Jeremy Isaacs' keynote MacTaggart Lecture, 'Television in the 80s'.[48] Soon after he gave up his position as Director of Programmes at Thames TV in 1978, Isaacs had started to be tipped as a possible future controller of a fourth channel,[49] and this speech was widely interpreted as an open letter of application for the job. As he put it: 'Those who argued for an OBA, who argued for pluralism as the best way to extend and improve British broadcasting, may have won the argument. They lost the vote.'

Isaacs described the fourth channel as one 'which extends the choice available to viewers; which extends the range of ITV's programmes; which caters for substantial minorities presently neglected; which builds into its actuality programmes a complete spectrum of political attitude and opinion; which furthers, in a segment of its programming, some broad educational purposes; which encourages worth-while independent production; which allows the larger regional ITV companies to show us what their programme-makers can do. We want a fourth channel that will neither simply compete with ITV-1 nor merely be complementary to it. We want a fourth channel that everyone will watch some of the time and no-one all the time. We want a fourth channel that will, somehow, be different.' The details of how these objectives could be achieved was a skilful summary of the middle-ground thinking on the topic but one which, for all its diplomacy, many felt erred on the side of caution. This was evident in his much quoted comment in discussion that the new channel would be different, but not *that* different.[50]

The government's thinking on what the 'strict safeguards' would be came soon after, on September 14, when the Home Secretary, William Whitelaw, spoke at the Royal Television Society's convention in Cambridge.[51] In what was, in effect, a mini-White Paper, Whitelaw pledged that the IBA would 'be expected to develop a distinctive service on the fourth channel. Within existing rules on taste, decency and the like, it should be designed to give new opportunities to creative people in British TV and to add new and greater satisfaction to those now available to the viewer. It will be expected to extend the range of programmes available to the public, to find new ways of serving minority and specialised audiences and to give due place to innovation. It will be expected not to allow rivalry for ratings between the two channels for which it has statutory responsibility nor to allow scheduling designed to obtain for each of these services the largest possible audience over the week'.

The Home Secretary said that the IBA would be required to arrange that 'the largest practicable proportion' of programmes came from independent producers, that the regional companies and ITN originated more material and, that the IBA would be further required 'in consequence, to ensure that those companies which have networking rights on ITV-1 have much less time on the fourth channel'.

He stressed that the IBA would be expected 'to ensure that the arrangements for planning and scheduling of the fourth channel service are not dominated by the programme companies contracted to provide programmes on ITV-1, especially the network companies. The arrangements for the acquisition and scheduling of programmes on the Fourth Channel will need to be separate from that for ITV'. The channel's income would come from spot advertising sold by the ITV companies, though block adverts and sponsorship would be allowed. The IBA would take enough money from the advertising revenue pool of both channels to provide the new output – the channel's income would not be solely tied to what its own advertising might raise. As well as a specific commitment to educational programmes, the service would be obliged to 'stimulate tastes and interests not adequately provided for on the existing channels'.

Now, with a Bill to establish the channel expected from the government in December, it only remained for the IBA to make its own conclusions clear. This it did on November 12 in a statement *The Fourth Channel. The Authority's proposals.*[52] Noting that its suggestions 'must of course be provisional, since final decisions rest with Parliament', the IBA expressed its concern to distance itself from the running of the fourth channel. It therefore planned to set up a separate company, with its own board of non-executive directors, chosen by the IBA after consultation. There would be an independent chair and deputy chair, 4 members from the ITV companies and 5 members able to speak for other potential suppliers, for example independent producers and those with educational concerns. The board would, subject to IBA approval, appoint senior staff, one or more of whom would be made executive board members. The company would also be a commissioning (not production) structure and would aim to construct a programme mix that was roughly two thirds 'addressing sections of the audience who want something particular or who want something different' and one third 'programmes intended to appeal to larger audiences, though often in a style different from that of some popular programmes now seen'. It was possible, the IBA felt, to use the scope of two channels to 'allow controlled encouragement to be given to the presentation of a wider range of opinions and assumptions'. As for how the two schedules would be related in practice, the IBA simply noted the need for 'co-ordination'.[53]

On the issue of programme sources, the Authority insisted that 'there should be no quotas, or rights to contribute, for anyone'. Nonetheless, it offered a possible division at the start of 15-35% independents, 25-40% major ITV companies, 10-20% regional ITV companies, up to 15% ITN, and 5-14% from foreign sources. All these would have a share of peak time. The IBA hoped that the channel would be on air at the outset or soon after for 45-50 hours per week. This would require an annual budget (to be decided by the IBA in consultation with the TV4 board) that was projected at around £60-80 million at 1979 prices, and this would come in the form of a Channel Four subscription from the ITV contractors. However, the IBA pointed out that it would 'not wish to see the Fourth Channel as a permanent pensioner of ITV-1: for the continuing health of the IBA's TV service, we should hope to see the Fourth Channel in due course adding between a fifth and a quarter, in real terms, to the total advertising revenue now earned by the programme contractors'. Finally, with its projected Autumn 1982 start in mind, the Authority intended to make special consultative arrangements during the early part of 1980 so that, when the Bill was passed, the channel could go ahead as quickly as possible.

The IBA's interpretation of the government's remit for a fourth service did not get an enthusiastic reception from the Channel Four Group. In October they had sponsored an open letter to William Whitelaw in *The Guardian* signed by almost 400 individuals and organisations inside and outside TV. This endorsed the spirit of his Cambridge speech and urged the IBA to meet its challenge which, it was argued, 'will demand a radically different approach to broadcasting in this country'. The Group also published its reply to the IBA's views on December 3.[54] They took particular exception to the suggested composition of the board, which gave 'a large measure of control' to the ITV companies – in direct opposition to the Home Secretary's expressed concern that they should not dominate the new channel's affairs. The Group, not surprisingly, also objected to the programme division of a maximum 35% for independents and the remaining 50-75% for ITV: 'The target for the Channel should be a minimum 51% of programme material to be supplied by independent producers'. If the independents should not in fact prove able to supply more than 35% at first, the Group argued, their share should be allowed to expand as the sector developed. The Group also continued to press their view that the IBA's concept of schedule 'co-ordination' gave the fourth service a merely reactive role.

These doubts about the IBA's plans were strengthened at the beginning of January 1980 when the ITCA's position on the fourth service became known. This emerged as a result of a leaked memorandum from the ITCA to the IBA, marked 'Strictly Confidential', and dated October 1979.[55] Its contents could be briefly summarised as a blueprint for an ITV-2, biassed substantially in favour of the ITV companies. Noting that 'there is already a large measure of agreement between the ITV companies and the IBA', it said that it was 'essential' that ITV was scheduled first and 'appropriate adjustments then made to assist the scheduling of the second channel'. The memo included a draft schedule which contained no significant traces of 'difference' or 'innovation' of any kind. The ITCA analysis of costs and income for the new channel showed an overall projected loss of some £8 million, based in part on what they termed 'an unforeseen increase in the ambition and hence cost of certain classes of independent programming', and they emphasised that, in their view, 'the financial viability of the new channel is far from assured. It will be a matter of necessity to maximise revenue and minimise costs'.

However the most memorable of the points made in the memo was about the name of the new channel. In a tone of brisk no-nonsense populism, it declared that since 'millions of television sets have for many years had ITV-2 on the channel indicator there is little doubt that, no matter what the official designation, it will be called ITV-2 by the public'. The fact that the major ITV companies had substantial interests in firms such as Radio Rentals, Rediffusion and Granada was left out of this tale of cause and effect.[56]

Channel Four on the statute book

The Broadcasting Bill was finally published on February 6, 1980,[57] and was drafted in the form of a set of amendments and supplements to the IBA Act of 1973, the principal legislation governing the activities of the IBA and its TV and radio programme contractors. It contained important provisions on a variety of topics apart from the fourth channel, but discussion here will only be concerned with Parts I and II, which provided the legal framework for the new service.

Part I, a single clause, extended the life of the IBA (which was otherwise due to expire on December 31, 1981) until the end of 1996. Part II, headed 'Provision of Second Television Service by the Authority', contained six clauses setting out the powers and duties of the IBA in providing Service 2. Limiting itself deliberately to a general statement of the main guiding principles, and leaving their detailed application to the IBA's administrative discretion, the Bill required that 'the programmes broadcast in Service 2 shall be provided by the Authority themselves', and that the activity of 'obtaining and assembling the necessary material' was to 'be performed by a subsidiary of the Authority formed by them for the purpose'. The IBA was also required to ensure that 'a substantial proportion of the programmes broadcast in Service 2 are supplied otherwise than by persons of the following descriptions, namely a TV programme contractor and a body corporate under the control of a TV programme contractor'.[58]

As for the character of the service, it was to be the Authority's duty 'a) to ensure that the programmes contain a suitable proportion of matter calculated to appeal to tastes and interests not generally catered for by Service 1; b) to ensure that a suitable proportion of the programmes are of an educational nature; c) to encourage innovation and experiment in the form and content of programmes, and generally to give Service 2 a distinctive character of its own'. Subject to this, the IBA was to maintain a proper balance within and between the two services. The programme contractors were to have the right 'in consideration of payments made to the Authority' to 'provide advertisements for inclusion in the programmes broadcast by the Authority in Service 2' for reception in their area. The income and expenditure of the programme contractors in connection with Service 2 was also to be taken into account in the calculation of their profits for the purposes of the additional payments (the levy) paid under the 1973 Act. Finally, the Authority was required to include in its annual report information showing how these responsibilities had been met.

The Bill's passage through the usual stages of parliamentary scrutiny[59] produced 21 separate occasions for debate, and the official Hansard reports of these proceedings run to nearly 800 pages.[60] However, although significant changes *were* made to parts of the Bill,[61] with one exception (discussed below) no changes were made to the clauses of Part II. The following discussion is therefore not a balanced summary of the whole legislative history of the Bill, but aims only to underline a few aspects with particular bearing on the preceding policy arguments.

During the Bill's passage the Labour opposition, led by Merlyn

Rees and Shirley Summerskill in the Commons and Lords Donaldson and Ponsonby in the House of Lords moved a large number of amendments to Part II. In most cases these were aimed at inserting further and more precise obligations on the IBA. Amendments were tabled to increase the scope for independent producers, strengthen the channel's independence from the ITV companies and clarify its editorial and financial position. Using its majority on the floors of both Houses and in Committee, the government was able to resist all these changes, clearly at odds with its declared concern to leave the details to the IBA. The only concession it did make was to accept the amendments, moved by Phillip Whitehead, to leave out all references to 'Service 2' and 'Service 1' and insert 'The Fourth Channel Service' and 'ITV'.[62] On this issue, although it did not need a vote, the opponents of 'ITV-2' won the argument.

The Second Reading debate in the Commons on February 18 was notable for two reasons. Firstly, Labour's formal amendments that 'this House declines to give a Second Reading to the Bill on the grounds that it does not provide for the institution of an Open Broadcasting Authority...' – lost by 139 votes to 177 – was the final parliamentary burial of this idea.[63] As Merlyn Rees put it: 'We shall not win on the OBA'.[64] The opposition would have to settle for encouraging the government to move in that direction from the starting point of a very different structure. Secondly, the Home Secretary, in his remarks opening the debate, explained the three fundamental factors which in his view made the OBA unworkable: 'First, I do not consider that the fourth channel should constitute a direct or continuing charge on public funds...The fourth channel... must be financially viable and self-supporting. There are, of course, risks with any new venture...but financial viability must be achieved and, if it is not, we shall be entitled to reconsider the future of the service. Secondly...I have always opposed the proposals for an OBA because I believe that there are risks in having an authority appointed and directly funded, to a substantial degree and on a continuing basis, by the Government. Thirdly, I should not be prepared to countenance a fourth channel that, far from extending the choice available to viewers, had the effect of restricting choice by intensifying to an unacceptable level competition for the ratings'.[65] Pressed by Clement Freud to say how long he would allow the channel to prove itself, Whitelaw declined to lay down a timetable: 'My only answer is "As soon as possible". I do not believe it will be very long'.[66]

There was one other discussion of special interest to this account. This took place in the final sitting of the Commons Standing Committee on the Bill on April 24.[67] As was mentioned above, the IFA had been arguing since the Edinburgh TV Festival for a Foundation to be set up by the channel to facilitate innovation and experiment, and at the beginning of February they had published detailed proposals.[68] This outlined a body at arms length from the main Channel Four board and disposing of at least 10% of the channel's budget. It was to have its own governing council of 12, made up of four members of the TV4 Board, four representatives of independent film-makers and four representatives of bodies such as the Arts Council, the British Film Institute, Regional Arts Associations and the TUC Arts Committee. The plan showed how the Foundation related to the existing infrastructure of independent film work, how this could be developed through a variety of funding mechanisms and set out the specific organisational forms which the sector's history had shown to be necessary if innovation and experiment were to be encouraged rather than just bought off or marginalised.

In the Committee Phillip Whitehead tabled a new clause and schedule to establish 'The Independent Programme Foundation' on IFA lines, and explained the case for it. Shirley Summerskill and a number of Conservative members also spoke in its favour. But replying for the government Leon Brittan, the Home Office Minister of State, said he shared the 'concern of the whole Committee that the fourth channel should encourage innovation and experiment' whilst insisting that 'the way in which it is done must be a matter for the authority and its subsidiary'. This meant that the IBA and the new channel 'will have to work out carefully how they will discharge a serious obligation imposed by Parliament with bipartisan support. The Government are entirely serious about the matter'. Having secured this statement of concern and a measure of support across party lines, there was nothing to gain from pressing the issue to a vote, and the motion was withdrawn. It was now another of the many questions that the Fourth Channel itself would have to resolve.

The end of the parliamentary process for the Broadcasting Bill – the consideration of amendments from the House of Lords – came in the Commons on November 10. These late afternoon exchanges were not well attended, a result of what Leon Brittan described as 'the excitement elsewhere in the building'. As Shirley Summerskill made a last unsuccessful attempt to tighten the duties laid on the IBA in its handling of programme contractors, the result was being announced of the latest contest for the leadership of the Parliamentary Labour Party. The winner this time was Michael Foot.[69] The Bill went on to receive the Royal Assent on November 13.[70]

Setting up the Company

As it had proposed in its November 1979 policy statement, the IBA appointed a panel of 'consultants' at the beginning of June and July 1980 who were to become the Channel Four Company's Board when the Broadcasting Bill became an Act. Headed by former Trade Secretary Edmund Dell and the film-maker Richard Attenborough, they included four representatives of the ITV companies and, to balance this, a further grouping of members who could represent the channel's interests in education, independent production and the broadcasting needs of Wales.

Their first major initiative was to advertise in July for a Chief Executive. At the end of September the Board announced that Jeremy Isaacs had been appointed to the post. They also announced another appointment. Paul Bonner, one of the applicants for the job of Chief Executive, had been made Channel Controller – a position not previously mentioned – with responsibility for the day-to-day scheduling and presentation of the Channel and in the acquisition of programmes.

With the Broadcasting Act in place, the Channel Four Company was formally established as a wholly owned subsidiary of the IBA. It was incorporated as a private company limited by shares on December 10, 1980. The Board of Directors of Channel Four held its inaugural meeting on December 17, when its terms of reference were presented to it by the IBA. (See Appendix 1). The Company came into operation on January 1, 1981, at which time Jeremy Isaacs took up his post. On January 5 Isaacs announced the appointment of three Senior Commissioning Editors – Liz Forgan (Actuality), Naomi McIntosh (Education), David Rose (Fiction) – and in mid-February the Board announced its appointment of Justin Dukes as Managing Director and Deputy Chief Executive. He joined Jeremy Isaacs in having a seat on the Board.

In April the channel announced its decision not to support the IFA's plan for a TV Foundation. The IFA had continued to campaign for this proposal, lobbying the Channel Four Board and publishing a further discussion paper 'British TV Today' in November 1980. In a letter to the IFA, Jeremy Isaacs explained that the Board had taken the view 'that such a Foundation was not necessary, and would risk replicating the bureaucratic structure of the Channel itself in funding film-makers. And the Board also considered that Channel Four should itself retain the right to dispense its own funds, and could not afford to set aside anything like so large a sum for independent work as your proposal suggested. The Board was quite clear, however, that the work of the film-makers you represent, although

CHANNEL FOUR TV – COMPANY STRUCTURE

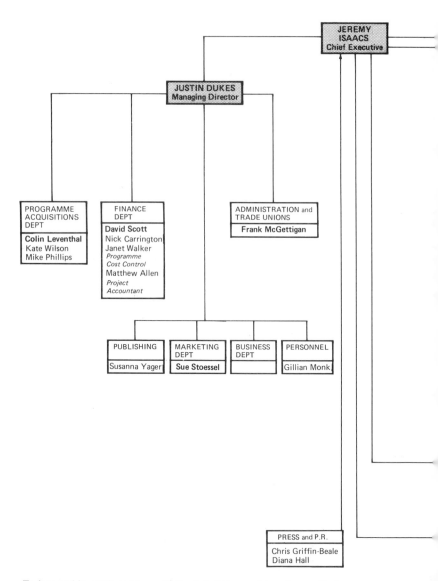

WILLIAM BROWN	ROGER GRAEF	DAVID McCALL	MANAGING DIRECTOR	ANTHONY SMITH	CHIEF EXECUTIVE

JEREMY ISAACS
Chief Executive

JUSTIN DUKES
Managing Director

PROGRAMME ACQUISITIONS DEPT
Colin Leventhal
Kate Wilson
Mike Phillips

FINANCE DEPT
David Scott
Nick Carrington
Janet Walker
Programme Cost Control
Matthew Allen
Project Accountant

ADMINISTRATION and TRADE UNIONS
Frank McGettigan

PUBLISHING
Susanna Yager

MARKETING DEPT
Sue Stoessel

BUSINESS DEPT

PERSONNEL
Gillian Monk

PRESS and P.R.
Chris Griffin-Beale
Diana Hall

To be read in conjunction with the brief biographies, Appendix 2

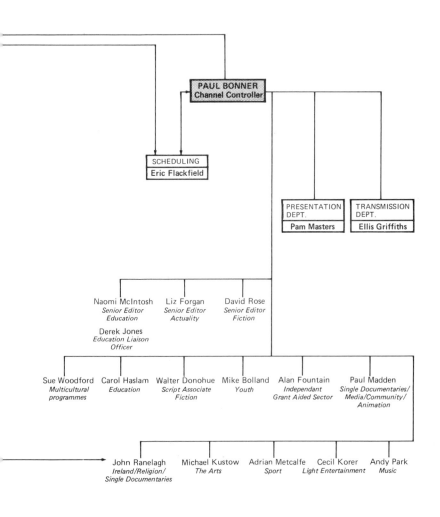

| EDMUND DELL | RICHARD ATTENBOROUGH | SARA MORRISON | ANNE SOFER | GLYN TEGAI HUGHES | BRIAN TESLER | JOY WHITBY |

PAUL BONNER
Channel Controller

SCHEDULING
Eric Flackfield

PRESENTATION DEPT.
Pam Masters

TRANSMISSION DEPT.
Ellis Griffiths

Naomi McIntosh
Senior Editor Education

Liz Forgan
Senior Editor Actuality

David Rose
Senior Editor Fiction

Derek Jones
Education Liaison Officer

Sue Woodford
Multicultural programmes

Carol Haslam
Education

Walter Donohue
Script Associate Fiction

Mike Bolland
Youth

Alan Fountain
Independant Grant Aided Sector

Paul Madden
Single Documentaries/ Media/Community/ Animation

John Ranelagh
Ireland/Religion/ Single Documentaries

Michael Kustow
The Arts

Adrian Metcalfe
Sport

Cecil Korer
Light Entertainment

Andy Park
Music

FILM PURCHASE
Leslie Halliwell
Derek Hill

having no exclusive claim on us, was fully deserving of our support. Instead of the Foundation, therefore, we propose the following: 1) to appoint a commissioning editor knowledgeable in, and sympathetic to, work being done by independent film-makers; 2) to provide funds to regional workshops on a bursary basis after publicly inviting applications for such bursaries; 3) to fund provision of additional facilities in at least two centres, one out of London, at which experimental programme makers can learn to use video equipment; 4) to commission, on its merits, the work of the best independent film-makers ... '.[71]

It was also announced in April that the Company – temporarily based at the IBA's London HQ in Brompton Road – was to have its own offices at Charlotte Street, London W1, on the site of 'The Other', and later 'Scala' cinema. When fully converted, the premises will include a presentation studio and viewing theatre, as well as the transmission play-out facilities. With alterations still in progress, the staff moved into the building in January 1982.[72] The process of making appointments, on both the editorial and administrative side, continued through 1981 and into the following year. At the time of writing (August 1982) nearly all posts have been filled, and the company has a total staff of about 90 people.

PART II　MONEY, PROGRAMMES, AUDIENCES

Channel Four's budget

The channel's budget is fixed annually by the IBA, after consultations with the Board. In their November 1979 statement the Authority suggested an initial sum of between £60-80 million per annum at 1979 prices. In a speech to the Royal TV Society in Southampton at the beginning of November 1980 Jeremy Isaacs had pointed out that 'every time I do the sums I find myself aware of how hard it will be to afford all that we want to do at that sort of budget.'[73]

At the end of July 1981 the IBA announced that Channel Four's operating budget from its inception up to the end of March 1983 was to be £104 million. This was divided into 2 parts: £18 million to cover capital expenditure, wages and initial programme costs to the end of March 1982; £86 million for the first year of full operation from April 1982 to March 1983.

At the same time the IBA announced the basis on which the initial phase of the ITV companies' 'subscription' payments for Channel Four were to be made. The new programme franchise for ITV (revealed by the IBA on December 28, 1980),[74] started on the

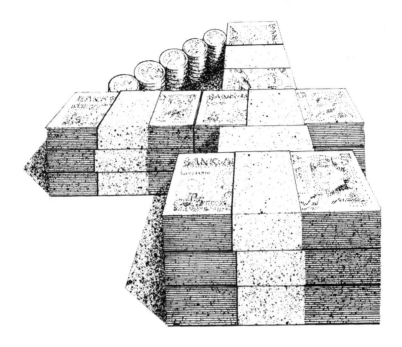

January 1, 1982, and all these contracts had been signed subject to the understanding that the companies paid a differential Channel Four 'subscription', set annually according to their own financial (calendar) year of January to December. The IBA's calculation of the Channel Four subscription for January to December 1982 was £98 million. But because of the special circumstances of that year, when advertising revenues from Channel Four would not be available to the companies until the end of the year, the IBA proposed to make up this sum in two ways. The actual ITV subscriptions for 1982 (almost all of it payable after April), would be half this sum i.e. £49 million.

The other £49 million would be raised by the IBA itself through a bank loan. The 1982 subscriptions had been calculated to include the first interest payments on this loan. After January 1, 1983 all Channel Four's finance would be provided by the annual subscriptions. These would be noticeably higher than in the first year, as they would have to be of a size to continue paying the interest on the borrowed £49 million, and to allow for it to be repaid within five years.[75]

Advertising revenue

The money that Channel Four receives from the IBA to spend each year is, of course, only half the picture. We need also to look at how it will earn money for the ITV system. This will happen through the mechanism of the ITV companies selling Channel Four's advertising time. There are many factors affecting the conditions under which this operation takes place, and a detailed review of recent thinking and projections of the channel's likely performance as an advertising medium would involve extended analysis. Instead, what follows is restricted to setting out the main indicators of the channel's performance and some of the key constraints in achieving its proposed targets.[76]

1. *Weekly Reach*

This is the proportion of the population who will view the channel at all over a week. In Channel Four's case a complication is introduced because at first the service will be available to only[77] 87% of the UK population, though this will rise rapidly to 94% by the end of 1983.[78] So at first the service will have a slightly reduced reach, but it is expected to compare well with BBC-2, getting a weekly reach in the 70-80% range. The channel will be a mass medium 'for all of the people — some of the time', as their brochure has it.[79]

2. *Audience Share*

This is the percentage of the population's total amount of viewing which is devoted to each channel. Channel Four plans to gain an approximately 10-15% share, mostly taken from the BBC channels and ITV (it is not expected to greatly increase total viewing). Total TV viewing per person in the UK now averages around 20-24 hours a week: if it reaches its projected share the channel could be watched for an average of 3-4 hours a week.

3. *Audience Composition*

The channel is under a statutory obligation to cater for 'tastes and interests' not generally served by ITV. It will be showing programmes addressed to the young, the old, ethnic minorities; programmes about 'leisure' and 'specialist' interests (e.g. basket-ball). Just who will watch these programmes is a more difficult question. Although the viewing patterns of UK TV audiences do show some variation by age, gender, class, and region, these gradients are not particularly pronounced: in Channel Four's case some of its programmes may tend to have a slight audience bias towards so-called

social classes ABC1. In general (and in contrast to the highly seg-
mented readership found for print media), it is likely to share the
rest of television's characteristics of low levels of loyalty to particular channels and to programme types.[80]

Even if the channel does succeed in attracting more attention
from large sub-sections of the population like 15-30 year olds, it
seems likely to have more problems with the 'specialist/interest'
categories. Assuming that such groups of gardeners, tennis-players
etc. *are* motivated to watch 'their' programmes on a regular and
sizeable basis, existing audience research will need to be extended to
detect these shifts, and to provide the detailed information necessary to convince advertisers that the channel is 'delivering' enough
of the right kind of viewers to make TV advertising (rather than
'specialist' magazines) a worthwhile proposition.[81]

If the channel does manage to reach its targets, and to reach
them in a steady and predictable way, then it should be in a good
position to attract substantial extra revenues. Contrary to the IBA's
expectations in 1979, ITV advertising revenues have been very buoy-
ant. They rose by 32% in the final quarter of 1981 compared with
the last quarter of 1980, and 1982 has seen this upward trend
broadly substained. The ITCA announced that the total revenue for
the half year to July 1982 had risen by over 16%, and an overall
increase of about 15-20% for the whole of 1982 is considered possible.[82] In the slightly longer term (the next 2 years), advertising
expenditure as a whole is predicted to grow 'quite rapidly',[83] and
commercial TV should certainly maintain its share (27% in 1980) of
this expanding total, and may be able to increase it a little. ITV
revenues for 1981 as a whole were over £600 million, and if the projections above hold up, the 1982 total should be in the region of £700
million. On a 10% audience share, these figures make Channel
Four's prospects of 'viability' in terms of net extra revenue to ITV
as a whole seem at least reasonably good. One recent forecast, prepared by Harold Lind and published by Channel Four itself, certainly points in this direction: it projects a net revenue for the
channel of over £100 million at 1981 prices by 1984.[84]

This sort of optimism may not be justified. It can be argued that
Channel Four will not achieve a 10% share for several years. It took
BBC-2 – the nearest comparable example – many years to achieve
this sort of audience share. Although hardly an unbiassed observer,
Alasdair Milne, the BBC's new Director-General has suggested that
'it is going to be extremely difficult to achieve the figure of 10%
within a year, a figure that has been quoted ... My guess is that it
will be 7, 8 or 9 years before they achieve 10% of the audience – and
there are plenty of people in ITV who agree with me on that'.[85]

Michael Ryan, a market research consultant, has also offered the following points about using BBC-2 as a model: 'Three assumptions are being made – 1) that in November 1982, when Channel Four is launched, BBC-2 will quietly disappear off the air and its audience will immediately transfer itself to Channel Four; that Channel Four's programmes will match the audience levels and demographic selectivity of BBC-2's, despite the fact that it took BBC-2 eleven years and one ITV strike to achieve their present level. 2) That Channel Four's programme ratings and their demographic compositions will be known in advance to agency time buyers. This is like winning the football pools by filling in the coupon after the results are known. 3) That knowing the said ratings and demographic compositions, time buyers will be able to buy the optimum schedules. This is like buying all the most desirable lots in an auction at the reserve prices.'[86]

Programmes

The amount of independent production which the channel has commissioned has been higher than expected. By the end of May 1982 416 projects from independent sources had been commissioned, and according to Channel Four these represented a rough parity of supply with the ITV companies. Not all the independent work will turn up in the first year's schedules. The company's estimates of output in the first 12 months of transmission are: 30% independents, 40% ITV/ITN (of which 10% will be repeats from ITV), and 30% acquired material (which is likely to include a significant amount of independent work, thus adding to the independents' overall share).[87]

One reason for this shift towards parity is probably the greater willingness of independent producers to run the risks involved in working with the programme finance that Channel Four is offering.[88] The level of its annual budget has meant that the average amount available for 1 hour's programme material is approximately £30,000, generally agreed to be a low figure by industry standards. Some prestige projects will be getting more than this of course, but others will be done for much less.

The main organisational focus for programme policy is the 'Programme Committee'. This usually meets on Monday afternoons, and is attended by Jeremy Isaacs, Paul Bonner, the commissioning editors as needed or available, and Colin Leventhal and others from Programme Acquisitions. Most proposals coming from the commissioning editors which get funding go through this committee, though not all. It can be sufficient to ensure the backing of Jeremy Isaacs or Paul Bonner – at any rate, no project is at all likely to get through without their support, especially that of Isaacs. The same applies to purchased material such as feature films.

Scheduling

Central to the decisions about the Channel Four schedule is the IBA's commitment – which goes back to their *ITV-2* paper outlined earlier – to a complementary relationship between the programme streams of ITV and Channel Four. The Authority set out what it meant by 'complementarity' in their November 1979 statement: 'It will provide as far as possible a choice at any one time between 2 programmes appealing to different interests: it means also that both the Fourth Channel and the present ITV service will be able to schedule programmes with less concern than is possible on only a single channel, especially in peak time, about potential loss of a majority of the audience . . . Our wish is that the Fourth Channel will take particular advantage of this freedom, and that enterprises and experiments will flourish'. Even so, they pointed out that 'it would be quite wrong on at least 2 counts to deny to the new channel programmes likely to draw very large audiences. First there is the need to lodge the service in the consciousness of the public . . . it must remain in the public's mind as accessible. Only so will it carry audiences over to some new and unexpected interests. Secondly there is the need to present the work of independent producers within a popular context rather than simply as a fringe activity'. In a brief Programme Policy statement of December 1980, which accompanied the Channel's terms of reference complementarity was defined by the IBA as: 'the provision of reasonable choice between 2 schedules, with a number of common junctions, and the co-ordinated use of the 2 schedules in the best interests of the viewer'.[89]

These commitments have a number of practical consequences. Firstly, they mean that, as far as possible, ITV and Channel Four will not schedule their high audience-rating programmes *against* each other. So, for example, Channel Four's proposed schedule from 6.30-8 pm will be mostly made up of educational programming and ITN's news hour.[90] This will provide an alternative for those viewers who do not want to see *Crossroads* or *Coronation Street*, nor the BBC's early evening offerings. Conversely, Channel Four plans to show comedy material from 6-6.30 pm, when most ITV contractors schedule their regional news.

Secondly, aiming for a number of common junctions simply means getting a proportion of the programmes to start or finish at the same times on the 2 networks, thus helping the viewer who decides to switch channels.

To the extent that 'complementarity' works, it should help to increase the total audiences for commercial TV. From Channel Four's perspective a substantial part of this audience is likely to be 'fugitive' viewers switching over for its films, sport and light entertainment when there is 'nothing much on' BBC or ITV. The marked tendency – when presented with 2 or more channels – for the audience to zig-zag through the schedules, picking out the less demanding programmes, has been noted by research done in Sweden, and has been called 'slaloming'.[91]

Towards a different future?

The channel will go on the air on November 2. By then, about £2 million of pre-launch publicity will have been spent to bring its arrival to the attention of the general public. A new national TV network, broadcasting for around 60 hours a week is, after all, quite a rare occurrence. The inevitable avalanche of comment, speculation and instant opinion will need to be kept in perspective. Even a short-term assessment of how 'well' or 'badly' the new service is doing will not be worthwhile until the Spring of 1983. The most prominent framework on offer for judging the 'success' or 'failure' of the Channel will doubtless come from the ITV companies. Against this it will be necessary to provide an *alternative* set of criteria for considering the channel's performance – a task which this book is designed to facilitate.

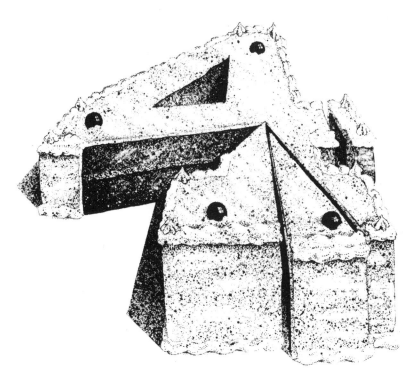

Channel Four
in Wales

The historian John Pocock has justly argued that British history is too serious a matter to be left to the English, that in fact it cannot be written, as it generally is, in purely Anglo-centric terms; ones in which the non-English parts of Britain are either ignored or alternatively, noted only as they affects matters of concern to the Imperial Parliament at Westminster.[1] In the next two chapters the historical background and future prospects of Sianel 4 Cymru (the Welsh Fourth Channel) are set out separately from the analysis of Channel Four in England Scotland and N. Ireland, in recognition of a distinct history. It will be part of the work now on the agenda to bring these two histories into new kinds of alignment.

Both chapters raise questions about the exercise of state power, national sovereignty, and the rights of linguistic and cultural minorities. Angharad Tomos gives an account of the struggle over the last 20 years, centred around *Cymdeithas yr Iaith Gymraeg* (the

Welsh Language Society), to get a comprehensive Welsh broadcast-ing service, directly accountable to the people of Wales. Jonathan Coe puts the structure of S4C into the context of the existing broad-casting organisations in Wales, maps out some of the problems the new Authority has faced with its programme suppliers, and assesses the advantages and drawbacks which frame its future.

Realising a dream

Angharad Tomos

The glass door was smashed. A watchman appeared, saw four youths breaking and entering the transmitting station, panicked and fled. The youths, two boys and two girls, ran the other way. They tried one room, then another, saw a main switch and turned it off. For a brief period on March 7, 1977 the television programmes from Winter Hill Transmitting Station in Manchester were stopped.

After being kept in custody and questioned about explosives and IRA connections, the four youths eventually appeared before the magistrates. In explanation, they said that they were members of the Welsh Language Society campaigning for a Welsh Television Channel.

If you were English, faced on that bench with such a claim, what would your reactions be? The magistrate's reaction was straightforward. Never having heard of the Cymdeithas yr Iaith Gymraeg – Welsh Language Society – nor any claim for a Welsh Television Service, he sentenced one girl to prison for six months, because of her record, and the others to six months each, suspended for two years.

If you were one of the Welsh youths in that dock faced with such a sentence, what would your reactions be? Their reaction was simple. They had done their duty, the protest had succeeded and the three returned home to Wales to plan further attacks on TV transmitters. The fourth member was delayed at Risley Remand Centre, but after four months she too returned to Wales to carry on the fight.

For ten years, this was the recurring pattern of the campaign for Welsh television. It was a simple battle fought face to face in the law courts – Welsh campaigners being 'sent down' by the establishment only to spring up again with renewed energy. Sianel Pedwar Cymru or S4C as it is known, the Welsh Fourth Channel Authority, was not the result of extensive debates and government reports and committees. It was the prize of a tooth and claw battle all the way. The government and broadcasting authorities did not want a Welsh Television Channel. The Welsh did.

Language as a battle-ground

Welsh is in fact one of the oldest living languages in Europe, although in 1536, a king of Welsh descent, Henry VIII, to all intents nullified the language by declaring that anyone who aspired to a position of office must be English speaking. As a result of this relegation from official recognition, the percentage of Welsh speakers in Wales today is only 20%. So on the grounds of statistics alone, Welsh speakers would seem to have no claim to a TV Channel for themselves. A whole channel mainly to cater for just 600,000 people is slightly ridiculous. And the fact that they *did* secure one in the end shows the depth of the commitment of Welsh speakers to maintaining their own national language and cultural identity.

It is a conscious act of will to be Welsh. The average Welsh child is brought up to be Welsh until the age of 11. They are Welsh at home and in their village or street. But as soon as they enter the secondary school, one of the most influential arms of the State, it is drummed into them that they are 'British'. Their Welshness mysteriously disappears, and is stored away in the mind of the average Welsh person along with other fond reminiscences of childhood.

One has to understand this strange dichotomy when discussing politics in Wales. To enter the mind of the thinking Welsh person is to be in a permanent state of 'double-think', caught between what the state tells you to think, and what you as a Welsh person really think. Left to the individual, probably all that would eventually remain of 'Welshness' would be a few nostalgic complaints in the form of ballads.

But in 1925, tired of British political parties, the Welsh Nationalist Party (now Plaid Cymru) was formed. This was radical from the outset. Nothing compared with the fervour of its Irish counterparts perhaps, but for Wales it was revolutionary in concept. Eleven years later a singular protest was made which had a permanent effect on politics in Wales.

In the Llyn peninsula in North Wales, the furthermost corner of Wales and a bastion of the Welsh language, the government proposed to establish a bombing training school. Fierce protests were made and there was strong campaigning against the proposal. But the government took no notice and the building of the training camp went ahead. Then one night in 1936 a section was burnt to the ground. The arsonists were no youthful rebels – one was the founder of the Welsh Nationalist Party, Saunders Lewis, a university lecturer; the second was a Nonconformist minister and the third was a schoolteacher. After setting the place alight they gave themselves up to the police. When the local Crown Court failed to agree on a verdict (which shows something of how the Welsh regarded their political 'criminals'), the case was transferred to the Old Bailey. They were found guilty and sentenced to nine months imprisonment.

The Welsh Language Society itself was formed in 1962 after Saunders Lewis gave the now historic radio lecture 'Tynged yr Iaith' – The Fate of the Language. In it he warned the Welsh that their language would not survive for long unless some action was taken to safeguard it. He took as an example the seven-year battle of a South Wales miner and his family who had campaigned to get tax forms printed in Welsh. Once again he stressed the need for sacrificial action – which could mean court hearings, fines and ultimately prison sentences. And although safeguarding a language's future may not appear to be the most revolutionary action, in Wales, the Welsh Language Society soon became an alternative to orthodox politics.

Its first major campaign was for Welsh road signs. English road signs were at first painted over and later removed altogether. The Society's aim here was to give Welsh its proper status in all walks of life, not just the small degree of recognition it received in the academic world of museums and libraries. For in most day to day institutions such as the Post Office, television or education, the medium was always English.

In 1968, the Welsh Language Society therefore started to call for more Welsh on television and radio. Not content with verbal opposition alone, it was involved in direct action right from the start. Its first step was organising a petition and rally in Cardiff along with protests on BBC premises in Cardiff and Bangor.

The background to this was that in the early 1960s the Pilkington Report had taken up complaints about the lack of Welsh on the media. As a result, BBC Wales was set up in 1964 and things improved. But by the end of the 1960s any progress had come to a halt. Discontent was even voiced within the BBC and IBA about their own programmes, and it was then that the WLS started talking about the idea of setting the 4th Channel aside exclusively for Welsh language programmes. It is difficult now to estimate how radical this suggestion was. But the authorities' immediate response was that such an idea was not only impractical, but technically impossible. They even detailed the impossibilities.

Fighting the 'impossible'

Nothing could have given more of a challenge to the WLS. If the State declared the idea impossible, the Society was bent on making it possible. Its job was making dreams come true. In 1970, the Society therefore formed a group whose sole purpose was to conduct a campaign for a Welsh TV Channel. This group met regularly, drew out its own TV policy and published it. It then set about to make this policy a reality.

In the booklet 'Broadcasting in Wales – To enrich or destroy our national life?', under the heading 'The Moral Function of the Broadcasting Media', the Society's position was clearly stated:

It would appear that the function of radio and TV programmes is two-fold; firstly they should reflect the spirit, civilization and life of the nation, and secondly they should enrich that civilization and enable the people to develop their own particular genius. Applying this to programmes which are broadcast in Wales, we find two obvious implications. They should make full use of Welsh – which is the national language of the Welsh people . . . Secondly, the programmes should be of Welsh material and putting forward a Welsh viewpoint . . .

In reality, English is the language of broadcasting in Wales and TV and radio sets are being used to Anglicise our homes and kill our language. A Welshman is thus educated to look at life through English eyes. The few Welsh programmes cannot do more in emphasising the idea that Wales is a small, insignificant province of England.

It is interesting to note that the campaign throughout was not fought in terms of the rights of cultural and linguistic minorities within the UK. Rather, the WLS repeatedly emphasised the rights of the Welsh people to a TV channel on the grounds of their Sovereignty – a sovereignty not recognised by the British government.

One of the Society's first difficulties was to draw attention to its campaign. Campaigning against the media has obvious drawbacks, and the media's unwillingness to give publicity to the WLS proved a major disadvantage during the first years. But drawing on its own resources, few as they were, the Society launched its campaign of educating the public with rallies, leaflets and petitions. Often the plans were quite elaborate, such as a walking tour through North Wales with night vigils on the way – and ending at the BBC premises at Bangor where TV licences were symbolically burned – followed by a week-long national tour on foot through Wales ending with a three day fast.

Resources were too limited to make these protests really effective. Yet the reaction of the Welsh Council on Broadcasting to the Society's booklet was at least favourable. The BBC administrators in London also asked officials in Cardiff for a report on 'the trouble concerning broadcasting in Wales'. Things were moving, and in its monthly magazine for April 1971 the Society said:

After Easter, we shall be in a strong position to proceed to the final stages of this part of the campaign. By then, we will have prepared ourselves and prepared a firm foundation for our cause and everyone will realise that every constitutional method has been tried. The results of interrupting broadcasting services and interfering with the authorities' property will be serious. Let the preparations be made, the rest depends on the will of our members.

Brave words, but before the year was out their author was facing two years' imprisonment for causing damage to broadcasting equipment.

This change in the WLS' tactics came about because it realised that it was not going to be the mass movement it had hoped for. So either it would have to be less extreme in its methods and gain more public support – or it would have to be content with being a small minority group using more extreme methods. The latter path was chosen, though unwillingly. It seemed that if the Society was to have any real impact in the TV campaign it would eventually have to resort to damaging property.

Direct action

Causing damage of any kind was totally contrary to the members' upbringing and background. Apart from the one major event of the Llyn bombing school and the recent examples of bombing, Wales has had no contemporary tradition of armed struggle. Due to the influence of Nonconformism, the political tempo was totally different to that of Ireland. There had grown up in Wales (with the success of the Labour movement in the early 1920s) a tradition of working from within the system. Wales' foremost political figures were prominent names in Westminster and the middle-class intelligentsia had all to lose and nothing to gain by following such a path. Many of the graduates or would-be graduates that made up the Society's membership could hope for promising careers within the establishment. Any kind of criminal record would seriously reduce their chances. But regardless of this, they started on the difficult path of damaging other people's property.

The Society's members came to look at damage to property in a new light. They were taught that English Law was almost totally based on property and this almost sacred view was mainly responsible for the capitalist system of the United Kingdom. But, they were also taught, there was a higher law that did not put the same stress on property – and that was the moral law. And on the grounds of moral law, it could be argued that one had to damage property to prevent damage to the language.

I believe that damage to property, under special circumstances, is totally in accordance to these principles and it is our responsibility to act on these principles to prevent violence – in this case – violence against the language and personality of Wales by England's broadcasting authorities ... It would be totally unjust to use personal violence against the body or personality of a broadcaster ... but it is totally just and in fact it is the responsibility of a conscientious Welshman to damage the instrument that is used to violate people.   – Ffred Ffransis, Mold Crown Court, 1971.

The first serious damage to television property was in Manchester in 1971, when three men broke into a Granada TV studio and caused 'limited damage' to television equipment. They damaged one television set considerably, scratched the lens of a camera and left the rest of the equipment untouched. The three then waited for the arrival of the police before eventually being brought to Crown Court. In court, however, the damage caused was estimated at £5,000, and two members were sentenced to twelve months imprisonment whilst the third, Ffred Ffransis, received two years in prison for breaking a suspended sentence.

'Welsh Channel: the only answer'

Throughout 1971 and 1972, the protests continued. TV masts were climbed, offices occupied, parliament interrupted, roads blocked. Members fasted, campaigned, took action, were tried and imprisoned.

At this time, the percentage of Welsh programmes on TV and radio was only 4.6% of the total output. The Broadcasting Council and the heads of both the BBC and Harlech Television used the excuse that increasing the number of hours of Welsh programmes would delay the work of improving reception. But the Society at this stage was more concerned to present the concept of an independent broadcasting Authority as a viable proposition. Critics suggested that while the system remained intact (with the BBC and an independent television contractor), all the WLS was doing was tinkering with the medium. Yet there was far more at stake than just the language in which the programmes were broadcast.

It is obvious that a Welsh Channel is not the ultimate aim of our campaign, but rather a Broadcasting Authority for Wales with total control over radio and TV services in our country. This Authority would be funded partly by TV licences and advertising profits and partly from Government funds. It would have the facilities to produce programmes and to adapt programmes from other countries, in both Welsh and English, to be broadcast during peak hours. Under this system, the Welsh speaker would receive a full service in his own language and also the non-Welsh speaker could look at Wales and the world through Welsh eyes in a language understood by him.
    – Editorial in *Tafod y Ddraig* (the WLS monthly magazine).

It was in January 1973 that Ffred Ffransis was released – after spending the best part of two years in gaol following the Granada damage – and there followed three months of intensive action by the broadcasting campaign. Much preparation work had already been done on potential targets, as well as securing enough members willing to undertake the task. And during the three months, WLS members interrupted programmes in Birmingham, damaged BBC vans in Cardiff and Manchester – and were imprisoned.

The Society's discontent was expressed at this time quite clearly:

Let us continue refusing to pay for our TV licences, and get more people than ever to join us in this important fight. Let us ensure that the Broadcasting Authorities receive letters from us as individuals and from societies and institutions of all kind – petitions, great and small, telephone calls and telegrams. Let us not give (them) a moment's peace; keep (them) awake night and day; let (them) know once and for all that here is a nation demanding a TV and radio service that could decide her fate.

WLS members continued to be in and out of prison throughout 1973 and 1974. Indeed this became a part of everyday life in Wales, with the regular appearance of people before magistrates for refusing to pay their television licence fees. There were hundreds of such cases – many people facing the magistrates on repeated occasions on these charges.

The Society's monthly paper was filled with discussions concerning the channel and speeches delivered by members in front of magistrates and justices – and after being released from gaol. The courts became the battleground of the language activists, and the battle was between English law and the Welsh language. Supporters and sympathisers were asked to be present when a 'language case' was on and this became a major aspect of the campaign. Often these cases made such an impact on those present, particularly the younger generation, that they were the deciding factor in their joining the WLS.

The authorities' response

By 1974, the Society had therefore gone a long way from being a voice in the wilderness. The campaign had attracted support first from nationalist organisations, then from religious denominations (who have far more influence on the social and political spectrum than they have in England). Eventually local and county councils followed suit and the campaign snowballed. But what was the authorities' response to this incessant pressure?

At the end of 1974, the Crawford Committee published its report on broadcasting. This recommended that money should be spent on a Fourth Channel in Wales to be on the air by 1976. Most importantly, it bore a remarkable similarity to the demands of the WLS. Its main recommendations were:

i.   A Welsh Channel broadcasting a minimum of three hours a night and 25 hours a week.

ii. The Channel would be under the control of a joint committee of BBC and HTV representatives.

iii. There should be a joint arrangement between BBC and HTV to share studios and staff.

iv. Welsh programmes should remain on the existing channels until the fourth channel could be received by most people in Wales.

This was in fact the second time within two years that the government had received a report from one of its own committees which contained practically all the recommendations made by the WLS. The Society still reiterated its conviction that an Independent Broadcasting Authority was essential – an idea not contained in the Crawford recommendations. But in spite of this, the WLS Senate suspended all law breaking activities and called on members and supporters to pay their TV licences – in the hope that such moderation would bring recognition from the authorities.

But the months went by, the Crawford Report remained on the shelf, and WLS members inevitably came to the conclusion that no direct action meant no government action. The only step the then

Home Secretary, Roy Jenkins, had in fact taken since Crawford was establishing yet another working party to look into the technical implications. Three months were given to complete the report, yet nine months went by and nothing happened. The WLS decided to resume its campaign of direct action.

Twelve months after being set up, the Siberry Committee finally published its report, declaring that a Welsh Fourth Channel *was* technically possible. This was the first time that a government body had actually said this. The report also gave detailed recommendations on programmes. These included contributions of 12½ hours a week in Welsh, improving the quality and balance of programmes in Welsh and a larger proportion of drama and light entertainment – programmes which were conspicuously absent from Welsh broadcasting at the time. The Society's main complaint against Siberry, however, was the absence of any fixed date for establishing the Fourth Channel. If work was started immediately it would still be three years before the first programmes were screened.

In January 1976, members of the WLS interrupetd the House of Commons demanding an announcement of a date from the Home Secretary. The same week, members also interrupted BBC broadcasts in Wales. But the Society was reluctant to launch into full scale direct action once again and their main weapon was to ask people once more to refuse to pay for their TV licences. This was one of the few methods of protest which had persistent effect.

Still nothing happened. 'We support the idea of a Welsh Fourth Channel,' the government would say, 'it's just a matter of money.' But when the White Paper on Public Expenditure was published, there was no mention of the Welsh Fourth Channel. It simply wasn't on the government's list of priorities.

On February 19, 1976, the date on which the White Paper was published, the House of Lords was interrupted by WLS members. This prompted the then Secretary of State for Wales, John Morris, to issue a press release:

I know that both Welsh and English speakers will be disappointed by this news (postponing the Welsh Channel) but I believe that it will be understood for the moment that we must give overall priority to our programme for industrial regeneration, housing and other essential social needs.

This was the first time that the Labour government had recognised such social needs as essential and everyone knew very well that it had no policy whatsoever for regenerating the Welsh economy. It was just another bluff. The Secretary of State finished the press release with an unfortunate choice of words: 'I ask for your patience a little longer.' But after eight years of waiting the Welsh had very little patience left, and after making his statement, the Secretary of State hardly had any peace.

Back to sabotage

At the WLS annual general meeting in October, 1976 the Society passed the following motion:

We note that the Government has not decided on a date on which the work of the Fourth Channel should start. As we have not had any answer up to now, we call on the WLS to start a campaign of direct action which could mean occupying and causing limited damage to the property of the Government and the Broadcasting authorities.

In less than a month, four members were in prison again and the same lines of action were repeated.

Keeping all past history in mind, no one in Wales nor outside could feign surprise when on February 7, 1977 the press reported that damage estimated at £25,000 had been done to a BBC transmitter at Blaenplwyf, near Aberystwyth in West Wales. The WLS claimed responsibility – and indeed it was one of the most striking instances of direct action in the Society's history. The rule of taking individual responsibility was waived for once – purposely. As a result the society itself, rather than individual members, were to face conspiracy charges.

By May of that year, yet another government paper was published on broadcasting – the Annan Report – which concluded that the recommendations on the Welsh Fourth Channel could be fitted in with whatever happened in the rest of the United Kingdom. The promises from Westminster continued to flow:

...detailed plans for the development of a Welsh language service capable of implementation as money becomes available are well advanced. The plans will cover the construction of transmitters as well as other aspects such as the provision of additional staff and studios. We will make further statements as soon as possible. – Brynmor John, Home Office Minister

How does one campaign against such words? Everything sounded so well. It was just that nothing happened. Gradually, other societies and movements which had given vigorous support began to lose interest in the campaign. The Welsh Nationalist Party devoted its energies to the campaign of Devolution. It was the hardest period ever faced by the Society.

The WLS then made a spectacular show, reserving all its energies for one whole year to stage it. That show was the Blaenplwyf

Conspiracy Trial, when the chairman and ex-chairman of the WLS were charged with conspiring to cause damage to the BBC transmitter. The two accused members prepared for the trial by making a tour of West Wales, calling meetings to explain their cause, and when the week-long case was held in July, the nation's attention was fixed on it.

In his speech at the trial, the Society's Chairman summed up the nation's feelings on the question of the Channel:

... the answer time and time again is that we must wait. Wait for that which is owed to us as a nation. 'Wait for the Crawford Report' – and we waited. 'Wait for the Siberry Report' – and we waited. 'Wait for the Annan Report' – and we waited. 'Wait for the Working Party's Report' – and we waited. 'Wait for the White Paper' – and we waited. 'Wait for the Welsh Channel' – and we are still waiting! As it was said once, 'Justice too long delayed is Justice denied.' We are not only fighting for our rights; we are fighting against the passing of time that will make our rights meaningless.

Christmas 1978 saw not only the imprisonment of the Chairman and ex-Chairman of the Society, but also members on hunger strike. Five members went on a 100-mile protest walk from Blaenplwyf transmitter to Swansea jail bearing a Five Point Demand: 1) Legislation to establish the Channel during the next parliamentary session. 2) Adequate financing for the Channel. 3) The establishment of a Welsh Broadcasting Authority. 4) A minimum of 25 hours viewing at the outset. 5) A definite development schedule.

Tory backsliding

By 1979, Wales was all set on Devolution. With Labour desperate for votes in parliament, even the three votes of Plaid Cymru, it passed the Devolution Bill in April 1979 and directed the IBA to get on with the work of preparing transmitters for the Fourth Channel in Wales. But though the Bill was passed, nothing was done, the Labour Government fell and in May the Conservatives came to power.

The Welsh shuddered – for if Labour was apathetic towards the language, the Tories were downright hostile. The only hope they had to grasp was the rosy promises in the Conservative Manifesto:

There is a widespread desire in Wales shared by English and Welsh speakers to use the Fourth Television Channel for separate Welsh TV broadcasting, and there is an understandable demand for an increase in the amount of Welsh broadcasting ... We are anxious to see Welsh Broadcasting starting on the Fourth Channel as quickly as possible. We believe that this could be done more cheaply, simply and at least as quickly if both the BBC and HTV programmes are transmitted on the Fourth Channel.

A significant deviation from the previous government's recommendation was the manner of financing the channel: rather than being entirely government funded, the independent TV companies would carry part of the financial burden. But the rosy picture painted by the government was viewed with suspicion, Welsh hopes had been dashed too many times in the past, and the WLS continued its pressure. Following serious damage to a transmitter in Midhurst earlier in the year, there were even rumours of another conspiracy trial.

The rosy picture in fact soon faded. HTV struck the first discord. They wanted the Fourth Channel to become an ITV-2 and said they would put their Welsh language programmes on it. The BBC could put theirs wherever they liked. Within weeks, their challenge to the Government was echoed by the regional committee of the IBA. During the National Eisteddfod of that year, the WLS action was therefore spearheaded against HTV, with the Society winning over more people than ever from the moderate side.

As a result of the pressure applied by HTV and other independent companies, Home Secretary William Whitelaw (in a speech at Cambridge) made the surprise announcement that he had decided to change course on the Fourth Channel. He would now share the Welsh language programmes between ITV-2 and BBC-2. The Welsh listened to the news in disbelief. Whitelaw's recommendations of dividing Welsh programmes on to two minority channels were in all senses the worst possible solution. It would be even worse than the present arrangement! There was also the added insult that Whitelaw 'did not even bother to come over and tell us'.

Seeing all that they had campaigned for over ten years in danger of being thrown overboard, the Welsh reacted furiously. They saw the government's disdain towards the Welsh language so apparent in the blatant abandonment of their election pledge – in favour of vested interest – that more and more people joined the ranks of the WLS. But this time the Society did not have to turn to prison-tired activists: others came to make a stand.

On November 11, 1979 the Pencarreg TV transmitter in Dyfed was switched off. When the police arrived on the scene they found three middle-aged men patiently waiting for them. These were the new recruits to the language campaign. In court, their names were announced as Ned Thomas, senior lecturer in English at University College of Wales, Aberystwyth, former *Times* leaderwriter and TV critic; Dr Pennar Davies, Principal of Swansea Theological College, leading figure in Welsh religious life and a well-known literary figure;

and Dr Meredydd Evans, senior lecturer in the Extra Mural Department at University College, Cardiff and former head of light entertainment at BBC Wales. Such cases as these made news in other countries, and soon people outside Britain began to look at the situation in Wales with interest.

Meanwhile, the WLS continually stressed the urgency of the TV campaign, pointing to the gross inadequacy of present Welsh broadcasting. Out of the 133 hours viewing over the three days of Christmas, 1979, for instance, only *four* hours were in Welsh! By March 1980, as a result, a growing number of people were refusing to pay their TV licences.

The final push

But if William Whitelaw had shocked the people of Wales eight months previously, MP Gwynfor Evans dropped a bombshell on May 6, 1980. In an ultimatum to the government he announced that until they decided to establish a Welsh Television Service on the Fourth Channel – broadcasting a minimum of 25 hours a week during peak hours, under Welsh administration and starting before the Fourth Channel in the rest of the UK – he would go on hunger strike as from October 6. Whitelaw had said no to a Welsh channel, Wales had said yes, and its most prominent politician had now declared a hunger strike if his demands were not met. Almost overnight, Welsh people rallied under the Society's slogans 'Save Gwynfor' and 'Welsh Channel – Now'.

July saw the first of those who had refused to pay their TV licences in this part of the campaign sent to prison. These were in part ordinary people drawn into the campaign, and one cannot underestimate the local repercussions of these court cases and the eventual imprisonments. Hearing of students in universities being imprisoned was one thing; seeing your neighbour escorted off in a police van was quite another. July also saw the 'Pencarreg Three', as they were known, given fines of £500 each and £700 costs. A fund was launched and contributions poured in.

During the summer, Prime Minister Margaret Thatcher was foolish enough to make more than one visit to Wales, and the Welsh were ready for her. In Swansea, the joint anger over the TV issue and the mass unemployment forced her to make a rear exit from a conference hall escorted by a strong police contingent. In Anglesey, the assault was even more direct. The Prime Minister's car was mobbed and literally shaken by protestors shouting 'Save Gwynfor', 'Save Gwynfor'. Coverage on the British TV news

Gwynfor Evans, President of Plaid Cymru, sets out his case for a Welsh Channel.

programmes of this incident gave the rest of the United Kingdom a much needed sense that something was seriously amiss in Wales.

The WLS also continued doggedly with the campaigning. A dramatic ambush was made on the car of the Welsh Secretary, Nicholas Edwards, when he was visiting his constituency. Another trio of prominent Welsh figures broke into a transmitter station. Regular excursions to London were made to block roads, occupy offices and interrupt parliament. Rallies continued in Wales, TV masts were climbed, phone switchboards blocked, Conservative offices occupied and transmitters raided and damaged. To reflect the solid support from groups in all walks of life, specific protests were staged: one week, HTV premises were occupied by thirty mothers and young children to emphasise the need of the coming generation; the following week a similar number of ordained ministers made their own protest.

At the Eisteddfod, held in August, the situation reached flash-point. Scuffles broke out between protestors and the police when the Welsh Secretary's car was escorted onto the field. The mammoth HTV stand was an obvious target for protestors, and it was in front of this stand that Gwynfor Evans chose to make a memorable speech:

He (Whitelaw) has promised to establish a Welsh language TV service by concentrating Welsh programmes at peak viewing times on the Fourth Channel. Keeping such a promise, well within his power, is a matter of ethics, not of election politics.

I too have made a promise. I have said that if Mr Whitelaw does not keep his word by October 6th I shall start fasting on that day, and I will continue to fast until the Government redeems its promise. I hope to show that a Welshman's word is his bond.

Shortly after this there was another attack by the WLS on a TV transmitter, this time at East Harptree, Somerset. The Society's Senate accepted responsibility and the police once again set out to organise a conspiracy case. The WLS also brought its annual general meeting forward to September to prepare for Evans' fast in October. Two rallies were to be held in North and South Wales during the first week of the fast and there was to be a mass rally in Hyde Park, London at the start of the third week. The foreign press took up the issue and were critical of the government. Something had to be done to dampen the fuse. Three Wise Men went up to see White-law: they were Cledwyn Hughes, Labour's ex-Foreign Secretary; Goronwy Daniel, Principal of Aberystwyth University and influential civil servant and the Reverend Gwilym Williams, Archbishop of Wales. The government hesitated, waiting. In Cardiff, 2,000 people gathered at a South Wales rally. The government capitulated.

Fear of fasting

It was not any concern for Gwynfor Evans' life that had brought the government to its senses but rather their fear of what would happen if he did undertake the hunger strike and died. Even in the last hours, it was still no more than a dirty game of power.

Strangely enough, Wales' reaction to the victory was not what one would expect it to be. In the first place, many had worked unceasingly for months to plan the last stand; they reacted as if stunned. Even at the hour of victory, in a crazy way, it seemed that the government had won. The Welsh had transformed the campaign from simply one for a TV Channel to one of national revival. Being forced to draw back their plans for attack made it seem that the government had won a point even here. The Welsh were also too wary to shout victory. Having tasted bitter disappointment too often, they were not going to be deceived again. Would Whitelaw break his promise? Would the government do another U-turn? Nobody knew. Worst of all, in the following months, nothing happened. The WLS was left alone to face the costs and casualties of the campaign. In less than a month, Hywel Pennar (son of Pennar Davies, of the Pencarreg Three) was sentenced to nine months imprisonment at Cardiff Crown Court, on a conspiracy charge. In January 1981, the Society took a bleak view of things:

All that was won in September was the Government's original position in May 1979. No more, no less. In truth nothing has really been won, only a re-declaration of the Government's original policy. Plaid Cymru members immediately started paying for their TV licences – this was a fatal mistake. Three months have gone by and there has been no move by either BBC or HTV to discuss plans and prepare programmes that should be on the air by November 1982.   – Euros Owen, *Tafod y Ddraig*, January 1981.

Eventually, things began moving slowly. By March, the members of the Welsh Broadcasting Authority were named and Owen Edwards, then head of BBC Wales, was appointed Director of the Welsh Fourth Channel. The new channel was baptised 'Sianel Pedwar Cymru (Channel Four Wales) or 'S4C'. But the Society was still very sceptical and wary of every 'development' and made desperate attempts to keep the support that had grown so quickly during the previous twelve months. Sadly, the support withdrew as fast as it had grown. All the Society was left with was yet another Conspiracy Trial.

Following the attack on the TV transmitter at East Harptree in July 1980, the police finally brought charges against the Society's broadcasting chairman, Wayne Williams; Euros Owen, a 20-year old student and leader of the Society's broadcasting group and Arwyn Sambrook. And it was not only the seriousness of the charges that were disturbing, but also the sheer length of time that these members and their families were under stress. It was June 1981 before the Conspiracy Trial finally reached Bristol Crown Court.

In the end, Sambrook was given a six months sentence, suspended for two years; Owen, who had been kept in custody since April, was sent for an indefinite period of Borstal training; Williams was sent down for nine months. Owen was later given another period in Borstal and did not see daylight until April 1982. Williams was released shortly before Christmas 1981, but was immediately faced with difficulties in his job as a teacher. Anti-Welsh parents voiced their opposition to an 'ex-convict' teaching their children and succeeded in getting a High Court injunction barring Williams from his post for six months, without pay. His teaching competence was questioned by the Minister of Education and by a High Court Judge before he was allowed to resume his job. He was simply one of many who paid the price – the price for a Welsh Channel.

CHAPTER 3

Sianel Pedwar Cymru – fighting for a future

Jonathan Coe

It is often said by broadcasters – or rather by the administrators of broadcasting – that Wales is a broadcaster's nightmare. Its geography causes repeated difficulties with transmission. Anyone familiar with Wales will recognise an element of truth in that; but perhaps it's more pertinent to note that from the point of view of the people of Wales, the broadcasting institutions they are blessed with are a Welsh person's nightmare.

Commercial television, despite the lip service paid to notions of accountability by the IBA, exists to make money – and Wales' independent contractor, Harlech Television, is no exception.

HTV's Director of Programmes in Wales, Huw Davies, once said that his company was 'the true home of the showbiz tradition in British television. We have lived our daily lives in the company of Lew Grade and Sidney Bernstein.' HTV's original line-up included such luminaries as Richard Burton, Elizabeth Taylor, Stanley Baker, Geraint Evans and Harry Secombe, and perhaps the most telling comment came from Secombe, who said, 'If they don't get the contract they can always form a Glee Club.'

More fundamentally, commercial television in Wales has always been tied to the West of England. According to the IBA and HTV this is out of necessity, but the claim is disputed by Welsh language campaigners and programme makers alike. The Welsh side of HTV was in fact substantially stronger at the time of its original application for the franchise (in 1967) than it is now, and during the mid-1970s the balance of power within the company shifted decisively in favour of the West of England businessmen – whose commitment to Wales and the Welsh language has never been strong.

Until a seven year contract with the Welsh Fourth Channel Authority was signed by HTV in May 1982 the company's major resources also went to its production centre in Bristol, rather than to its desperately out-dated Welsh counterpart in Cardiff. Plans for a new Welsh HQ at Culverhouse Cross on the outskirts of Cardiff were delayed for many years, and lack of studio space today still curtails the company's contribution to S4C.

This Anglocentric view of broadcasting in Wales is one of the reasons why the ten year campaign for a comprehensive Welsh broadcasting service has by and large been ignored by the British media. Individual acts of resistance have attraced sporadic coverage as a series of sensational 'incidents'. But little attention has been paid to the substantive issues involved, and even the best reporting has tended to reproduce the stereotype of the 'lunatic Celtic fringe'.

Outside Wales many people have failed to understand how television could possibly be the source of such conflict and controversy. This incomprehension was most clearly manifested when Gwynfor Evans announced his hunger strike, which brought about the Thatcher government's capitulation. How could someone, it was asked, contemplate dying for television? In fact broadcasting in Wales has never really catered for the needs of Welsh speakers, who have continually had to *demand* recognition for their language. And when the authorities have responded, no matter how meagrely, English speakers in Wales have felt deprived. Few monoglots would deny Welsh speakers a service of some kind, but not if it means any sacrifice on their part.

Thus broadcasting, more than any other sphere of Welsh public life, has been the focal point of political and lingustic conflict. Successive governments have been content to leave the issue unresolved, watching the Welsh fight it out amongst themselves, and with few exceptions, the Welsh Labour establishment has willingly joined the Tories in exploiting the fears of English speakers.

It is important, however, to understand that the solution of Cymdeithas yr Iaith Gymgaeg to the problems of bilingual broadcasting, although originally dismissed as unworkable, eventually achieved almost unanimous support within Wales – and from both language groups. As Welsh Secretary Nicholas Edwards sadly admitted when announcing his government's second spectacular U-turn: 'We have failed to persuade middle-ground opinion and the media in Wales that our judgement was right.'

The Welsh Fourth Channel in action

Early in November, S4C will begin broadcasting just a few days before Channel Four is launched in England, Scotland and Northern Ireland. For the time time, Welsh speakers will also have an independent Welsh-language television service with an identity of its own. Welsh programmes will be removed from BBC Wales and HTV Wales, and non-Welsh speakers will no longer have to put up with programmes they don't understand.

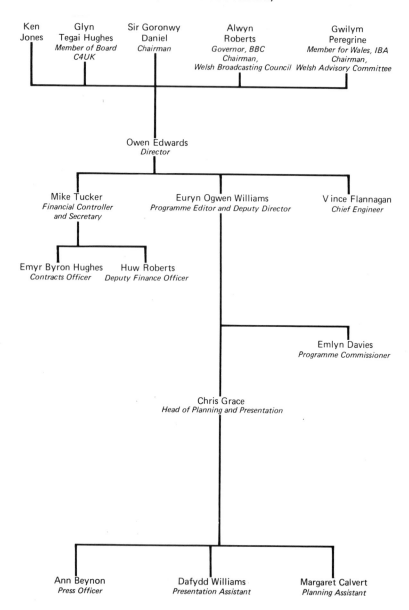

SIANEL PEDWAR CYMRU S4C
Welsh Fourth Channel Authority

Ken Jones
Member of Board C4UK

Glyn Tegai Hughes
Member of Board C4UK

Sir Goronwy Daniel
Chairman

Alwyn Roberts
Governor, BBC Chairman, Welsh Broadcasting Council

Gwilym Peregrine
Member for Wales, IBA Chairman, Welsh Advisory Committee

Owen Edwards
Director

Mike Tucker
Financial Controller and Secretary

Euryn Ogwen Williams
Programme Editor and Deputy Director

Vince Flannagan
Chief Engineer

Emyr Byron Hughes
Contracts Officer

Huw Roberts
Deputy Finance Officer

Emlyn Davies
Programme Commissioner

Chris Grace
Head of Planning and Presentation

Ann Beynon
Press Officer

Dafydd Williams
Presentation Assistant

Margaret Calvert
Planning Assistant

*Huw Morris Jones left this post in March 1982

To be read in conjunction with the brief biographies, Appendix 2

The control of this new station is vested in the Welsh Fourth Channel Authority, which consists of five people appointed by the Home Secretary. Three of them – Alwyn Roberts, Huw Morris Jones and Glyn Tegai Hughes – happen also to be respectively the chairmen of the BBC in Wales and the IBA's Welsh advisory committee, and a member of the board of C4UK. That apart, the organisation is unique in the history of British broadcasting. For although it will operate within the framework of commercial television and will be financed by the IBA, the authority is independent, breaking across the traditional divide between public service and commercial broadcasting.

S4C's commitment to Welsh programmes was laid down in the Broadcasting Act 1980, which stipulated that 'a substantial proportion of the programmes included in the programme schedules provided by the Welsh Authority shall be in Welsh; and the programme schedules shall be drawn up so as to secure that the programmes broadcast on the Fourth Channel in Wales between the hours of 6.30 pm and 10.00 pm consist mainly of programmes in Welsh.' When Welsh programmes are not being shown C4UK material will be broadcast, but S4C will draw up the timetable and choose which programmes to show.

The money for buying programmes and administering the new service – with spending on administration, building and presentation limited to £1½ million – will come from all the independent television companies, by way of the IBA. But although it will broadcast on a commercial channel, S4C will still be able to take programmes not only from HTV and the independent producers but also from the BBC.

S4C will not produce its own programmes, although it will have a small presentation department. Instead it will buy programmes from HTV and the independent producers, or from other English and foreign TV companies. BBC programmes will of course be paid for with money from the licence fee, and will simply be handed over to S4C for broadcasting.

The new arrangements have been described by Euryn Ogwen Williams, S4C's Programme Editor and Deputy Controller, as 'a partnership that depends on the will of the partners'. But though each of the partners have stated their own commitment to the success of the new service, the set-up is far from ideal. Owen Edwards, S4C's director, said discussions with programme suppliers progressed 'amicably and satisfactorily', but there were substantial problems.

On the surface, the relationship between S4C and the commercial sector – HTV and the independent producers – is clear: S4C buy their programmes and can stipulate what they want. Between them, HTV and the independents will supply 12 hours of programmes a week, HTV producing 7¾ hours and the independents 4¼. The independents started work as soon as was practically possible and have surpassed S4C's expectations. They will receive, on average, £28,000 per programme hour. HTV's preparations, on the other hand, were severely hampered by an argument with S4C about the exact meaning of 'commercial terms' – in other words how much they would get.

When the company initially asked for £53,000 an hour, S4C would have none of it. There followed eight months of often bitter arguments, at the end of which S4C and HTV finally agreed (in May 1982) on a mutually acceptable deal. A contract was signed to run from 1982 to the end of 1989. Divided into two main periods, the first will continue until HTV's additional production facilities have been built at Culverhouse Cross, probably in 1984. During this time the company will provide an average of 7¾ hours per week. After the completion of the new studios until the end of 1989, its supply will increase to 9 hours. The cost per hour was set at £34,500, rising to £35,790 in the second period.

Enthusiasm for these arrangements was not shared by all. Wayne Williams, a former chairman of CYIG, said that 'since it is likely to take two years or more to build studios at Culverhouse Cross it is totally unacceptable for S4C to talk of an increase of an hour and a half in Welsh programmes. S4C decision means the channel will not have reached that minimum even after almost three years of broadcasting. If this is S4C's idea of developing its Welsh service, there's something wrong somewhere and Cymdeithas will be pressing for an earlier increase.'

On the other hand the BBC, whose duty is to supply ten hours of programmes a week, is insisting on retaining editorial control – that is, deciding which programmes to produce. It is, of course, willing to discuss with S4C the kind of programmes that the authority would like, but if an argument is unresolved the BBC will always have the upper hand. As a result, if S4C, for whatever reason, refuses to transmit a programme offered to it by BBC Wales it will be left with a gap – and no money to buy programmes to fill it.

When it came to news and current affairs, S4C rejected the establishment of a 'Welsh ITN', as some groups who gave evidence to the select committee on Welsh affairs would have liked. Instead it invited both BBC and HTV to apply for the news 'franchise'. HTV pulled out before a decision was taken and the BBC was left with the franchise.

All power to the independents?

Assessing the preparations for S4C, *Y Cymro* (a weekly Welsh language newspaper) said that the most striking impression was the difference between 'the enthusiasm and energy of the independent producers on the one hand and the dawdling of the BBC and HTV on the other'.

From one perspective it's true that the most exciting development in Welsh language broadcasting is the work of the independent producers. The main producers will be Ffilmiau'r Nant (Wil Aaron), Ffilmiau Ty Gwyn (Gareth Wyn Jones) and Alan Clayton, Endaf Emlyn and Sion Humphreys. They will be assisted by the establishment of Barcud – an outside broadcast unit based in Caernarfon and with an editing and dubbing centre in Cardiff.

However, doubts have been voiced about the 'infectious enthusiasm' of the independent producers. On the one hand it is feared that the big money to be earned will attract people whose interest is solely financial. On the other, there are fears that the sudden expansion in this sector will open the door to the unprofessional – either by way of deliberate attempts to cut costs or lack of experience.

Euryn Ogwen, Deputy Controller of S4C, is aware of these problems but says he does not intend to give independent producers an unfair advantage over the BBC and HTV by cutting corners. Everything will be worked to union regulations, he says, and draws attention to the fact that the producers who have already made programmes have reached agreements with Equity, the actors' union, and the ACTT.

But there have already been some spectacular failures and Gwilym Owen, HTV's former head of news and current affairs, has been involved in two serious bungles. A major dramatisation of the Welsh classic *Madam Wen*, produced by him on behalf of Bwrdd Ffilmiau Cymraeg (the Welsh Films Board), was found to have exceeded its budget by probably as much as £150,000. S4C immediately announced an investigation and insisted that Owen be replaced.

At about the same time Owen was working independently on another project for a Welsh version of 'Question Time'. The authority turned the scheme down but did give approval in principle for a more light-hearted panel programme. S4C told Owen to send details of the format and budget, but the first thing they got were two completed programmes. Both were rejected and Owen left to foot the bill. But the greatest expense was the hiring of Barcud's outside broadcast unit – of which he was the managing director, earning £18,000. Owen resigned, claiming to have taken his decision for 'personal reasons'.

Transmission problems

The responsibility for transmitting the new Welsh service will be in the hands of the IBA. Wales was given priority in the building of transmitters for the new service, and the Mynydd Bach transmitter near Ystrad Mynach in Mid-Glamorgan was the first in Britain (in May 1980) to be equipped for transmitting the Fourth Channel. By November every one of Wales' main transmitters, along with 80 relay transmitters, will have been equipped.

But serious problems will arise in some areas where the relay transmitters will not be ready. Unfortunately, many of them are predominantly Welsh-speaking. Villages such as Bethesda and Waunfawr in Gwynedd will have to wait for as long as two or three years before seeing S4C. Not surprisingly, this has caused discontent and ill-feeling.

Another problem is cable television. Pontypool MP, Leo Abse, has pressed the Home Office to allow cable television operators to carry Channel Four UK rather than S4C. If he succeeds, this will cut S4C's potential audience considerably. Not only would S4C be competing on unfair terms, but Abse himself has been accused of trying to hamper the new channel's success before it even starts.

A provisional assessment

It is obviously impossible to adequately assess S4C before it starts broadcasting. Like any other channel, it must be judged by what it provides, not what it promises. But nonetheless some provisional assessment is necessary.

The advantages of S4C as far as Wales is concerned are as follows. For the first time ever there will be a unified Welsh language television service on one channel, with a commitment to expansion. Secondly, the removal of Welsh programmes from the main channels leaves space for an increase in English language, but Welsh-produced, output. Thirdly, the new Welsh Fourth Channel Authority need not always look to the ITCA or the IBA or the BBC in London, and can put the needs of its own audience first. Fourthly, the new system allows programmes to be obtained from sources other than the BBC and ITV. The independent producers by and large are based in North and West Wales and are closer to the Welsh-speaking audience – and this kind of competition might force the established producers, and HTV in particular, to improve their standards.

There are, however, drawbacks. Firstly, S4C is an 'experiment' which according to the government is to be reviewed in three years' time. Secondly, although 22 hours a week will be a major increase in Welsh programming, it is still a long way from what English-language speaking viewers would regard as a comprehensive television-service. Thirdly, some C4UK programmes (although mostly to be shown either at time of transmission or else rescheduled) will be missed, and the 'deprivation factor' which has been the root of the English speaker's discontent for so many years will still be there. And if the commitment to expanding Welsh language broadcasts from the 22 hours is honoured, this problem will be exacerbated.

Finally, and perhaps most importantly, S4C is hardly more representative than the existing broadcasting bodies: of the five members of the board, three belong to Wales' broadcasting establishment and as yet S4C has refused any suggestions for democratisation. It remains to be seen whether the political pressure necessary to force such a fundamental change exists.

Further reading

D.E. Thomas and Emyr Williams, 'Wales: Commissioning National Liberation,' in *The Bulletin of Scottish Politics* vol.1 no.2, Spring 1981.

Gwyn Williams, 'Mother Wales, Get Off Me Back?' *Marxism Today*, December 1981; and Dafydd Elis Thomas' reply in *Marxism Today*, March 1982

Gwyn Williams, 'Land of our Fathers,' *Marxism Today*, August 1982

Education, news, current affairs

The three Senior Commissioning Editor posts at Channel Four are those of Fiction, Education and Actuality (covering News and Current Affairs). We decided, early in the planning of this book that, since critical work on Television Fiction had been well represented recently (cf. *Screen Education* 35, Summer 1980; *Popular Film & Television*, T. Bennett et al (eds) BFI/OU 1981), we would concentrate on the two other areas – Education and Actuality.

Charlotte Barry examines the attempts being made by Channel Four to broaden the definitions of educational programming, to give it a higher profile in the schedules and to develop more 'interactive' relationships with audiences/users. She examines the ways in which the Channel's programming will tie in with institutions of formal and informal education, looks at questions of 'accessibility' and at how 'continuing education' might be understood.

Holly Goulden, John Hartley and Trevor Wright discuss the

pressures exerted on the Channel by the existing professional ideologies and institutions of news-making in the light of the decision to
award ITN the contract to provide the main news service. They
question the extent to which the 'new' news service can meet any of
the well-documented criticisms directed at TV news and current
affairs over the last ten years (for example, the work of the Glasgow
University Media Group, summarised in *Really Bad News*; Writers
and Readers Publishing Co-op, 1982).

Barry Flynn draws on his experience of working inside ITN to
contrast their routines and conceptions of newsmaking with the
strategies being developed by the Channel's 'Alternative' news
team, Diverse Production.

Lesley Hilton looks at the issues surrounding the allocation of
contracts for the channel's weekly current affairs programme, to be
produced by two separate companies – Gambles Milne Ltd and
Broadside – both run by women.

CHAPTER 4

Programming for Education

Charlotte Barry

Channel Four's education team intends to work along the lines of the famous lager adverts – refreshing the parts of the population that traditional adult and continuing education can't reach. At a stroke, the new channel will more than double ITV's educational output and uniquely, will show educational programmes at peak viewing times.

There will be no schools programmes and little for younger children. But instead, Channel Four wants to focus on education for adults in the widest sense, embracing everything from the purely intellectual to the practical. Some of the programmes could be so informal that they will be indistinguishable from the general output of news, documentaries, arts, light entertainment and sport.

The senior commissioning editor for education, Naomi McIntosh, a former Open University professor, wants programmes to be suitable for individuals or groups to watch either at home or in a more formal setting, like an adult education institute. 'Anything which people want to learn and which makes people want to learn should be part of our canvas,' she has said. 'Sometimes it may stimulate them into other activities, sometimes they could simply be wiser or better informed.'

Informal education

Naomi McIntosh's leaning towards a more informal approach characterises the changing attitude in adult and continuing education towards traditional distinctions of what is or is not educational, and it bears the stamp of the growth of the lobby for such changes over the last ten years. It also mirrors the introduction of many new and different ways of teaching adults that at long last got away from the rigid framework of night school, the university extension movement and the traditional approach of the Workers' Educational Association – which aimed to lift the worker intellectually above the drudgery of everyday life.

Things really began to move when the Open University was set up, against all the odds, in 1969, in order to provide correspondence degrees, backed up by television and radio broadcasts, weekly tutorials and summer schools, to anyone who wanted them. In 1972, the Russell Report in turn recommended a wholesale expansion of all kinds of adult education.

A major development from that report was partial Government funding for the adult literacy campaign through the Adult Literacy Resource Agency. One of the most significant educational innovations of the 1970s, this followed the British Association of Settlements' launching of the 'Right to Read' campaign, which sought to help Britain's two million illiterate adults. It also coincided with the BBC's plans to mount a three year television and radio project, and in 1975 the television series 'On the Move' began.

The 'On the Move' programmes did have some teaching content, but they aimed primarily to publicise the problem and encourage people to seek help. Within two years more than 100,000 students and 50,000 volunteer tutors had come forward. This proved to be only the tip of the iceberg.

Another of Russell's main recommendations was to set up an agency to coordinate adult education across the country. Five years later, a watered-down version was announced by the Labour Education Secretary Shirley Williams. The Advisory Council for Adult and Continuing Education was to promote 'accessibility as its keynote', encouraging cooperation and coordination between the many providers of adult education – from the university extra-mural departments to the Open University, from local authority evening classes to voluntary organisations like the WEA, literacy schemes and community education projects.

Unfortunately for Russell and the new advisory council, its establishment coincided with the gradual decline in public spending which led up to the savage education cuts of 1979. Adult education came worst off, largely because of its weak bargaining position. Local authorities are not obliged to fund adult classes, unlike schools, and this made it easier for them to cut back. Fees doubled overnight in some parts of the country, and a few authorities even tried to charge for literacy tuition or abolish concessionary rates to pensioners.

A relevant education?

In spite of the cuts, the general trend during the 1970s was to make adult education more accessible, less of a flower-arranging middle ghetto and more relevant to working class people, women at home with small children, the elderly, ethnic minorities, handicapped people and the unemployed. The broadcasting lobby followed this trend, spurred on by the success of the adult literacy campaign and the Open University. For the first time education broadcasts meant not just schools broadcasts or intellectual talks (like the Reith lectures), but a way of opening people's eyes and encouraging them to learn.

The Labour Government's 1978 White Paper on broadcasting officially recognised that education should have a 'significant place on the fourth service' and in this echoed the earlier Annan report. The response from the Advisory Council for Adult and Continuing Education, now with Naomi McIntosh as a leading member, was to remark quickly on the need for a follow-up or referral service, as pioneered by the BBC's adult literacy campaign. It also stressed the importance of appointing an educational liaison officer at the new channel to deal with adult education agencies and organisers in the field so that they could prepare materials and courses to coincide with programmes.

At the same time many adult education professionals expressed fears that existing broadcasting channels would see this as a green light to reduce their own educational output. This course was in fact attempted by the BBC early in 1980, but abandoned after adverse publicity. Certainly local radio stations, charged to include some education in their schedules, have largely chosen to ignore the requirement: their promise to contribute to political education has, resulted – as Dr. Tony Wright's research for the IBA showed – in disappointingly meagre public affairs programmes and precious little promotion of political awareness.[1]

There *have* been some success stories though. A series of discussion programmes on BBC Radio Ulster in the late 1970s called 'What is happening to us', for instance, formed an oral picture of the problems dividing Northern Ireland since the troubles began. The issues explored in the four 15-minute programmes were produced by a team from Magee University College in Derry, (the adult education wing of the New University of Ulster), in active cooperation with community, women and youth groups who helped to devise the format, gather material and write scripts. At the same time the Community Action Research and Education project set up discussion groups, provided back up materials and leaflets, though this was less successful.

Continuing education

It is precisely this sort of approach which Naomi McIntosh's team wants to use for education programmes on Channel Four. They have drawn heavily on the report prepared by her own committee for the Advisory Council for Adult and Continuing Education, 'Continuing Education: from policies to practice', which mapped out the course of education for adults until the end of the century.

The report says educational broadcasting should have five main functions. Programmes should be educative rather than educational, accompanied by special books and materials; be linked with local educational opportunities; provide teaching materials for tutors; and also produce total packages of broadcasts, cassettes, manuals and books – like the BBC's renowned foreign language programmes.

The report reiterates the importance of radio and television in education. 'Those who see no value for themselves in education can be encouraged through the educative and linking functions of broadcasting to reconsider that judgement,' it says. People unwilling or unable to have face to face tuition can learn in their own homes at their own pace and convenience. Valuable opportunities are being lost in Britain to build learning materials on general broadcasts of drama and documentaries, the report points out, and it calls for new legislation to clarify the copyright laws which restrict the educational exploitation of learning materials.

Bearing all this in mind, an important part of the channel's education service will be to give people the opportunity to pursue ideas raised in programmes in their own time. Derek Cook, the educational liaison officer, wants to make sure that no programme is allowed to go out without advance publicity and back up material. These will vary from simple leaflets, cassettes and books (but not the coffee table variety) to more complicated schemes involving colleges, adult institutes, voluntary organisations and community services. The possibilities have already been explored with health councils, Age Concern, the Adult Literacy and Basic Skills Unit and the National Federation of Women's Institutes.

As a result, the sort of thing about to appear on our screens is a weekly magazine for the over-60s, which will go out at tea time and could eventually be written, made and presented in cooperation with viewers. Another priority is a weekly series in the prime mid-evening slot for people wanting to learn more about their combined roles as parents, consumers, voters, taxpayers, trade unionists and bosses.

In cooperation with Carol Haslam, the other commissioning

editor for education, the team has also planned a series looking at the social, political and economic determinants of health, such as occupation, gender and social class. There are other series planned on social and cultural life in China, a history of Africa, technology since the Stone Age, and the 1960s.

In the area of formal education programmes, Channel Four will deliberately avoid languages, computers and adult literacy, all of which are already dealt with by the BBC. But it will balance this with its own adult numeracy series, intended to improve and build on the successful Yorkshire TV series *Make it Count* and *Numbers at Work*. The National Extension College in Cambridge will provide the back-up for the everyday maths programmes, including a computerised marking service similar to the RSVP system in the United States.

Channel Four has also been strongly lobbied for airtime for the Open Univesity, the new Open Tech (to provide specifically technical courses) and the revised youth training scheme sponsored by the Manpower Services Commission. So far, it has refused to take the overflow from the Open University's undergraduate programme (as it is pushed out of peak hours on BBC2), but may give space to its continuing education programmes for parents, consumers, managers and school governors. But the channel is more likely to allow the youth training scheme to transmit during the daytime, providing that one day is set aside for adult training projects, and give over Saturday and Sunday mornings to the Open Tech programmes.

The university of life?

So Channel Four's education proposals seem laudable enough on paper, but there are a number of hidden dangers. Concentrating on the 'educative' rather than the purely 'educational' could lead to the trap of calling everything education, from gardening to drama to the news headlines – the University of Life syndrome.

Attempts to follow up programmes could well turn out to be more difficult than the team envisages. It is easy to talk glibly about liaising with adult education providers up and down the country, but has the education team actually sat down and thought how to go about it in detail? Adult education is quite rightly varied, but also totally uncoordinated, and Channel Four may have difficulties in reaching every community education project from Stirling to Southampton. One danger is that the Channel will take the easy option and concentrate on the larger agencies and the few local authorities which are willing or able to foot the bill for back up materials.

In this context Channel Four may well have some things to learn from the experience of the Open University (OU). One such problem – which has led some people to question the suitability of the word 'Open' in the OU's title – has been its failure to reach working class people in any large numbers. From the start the OU has attracted large numbers of middle class students, mostly women at home or teachers and middle managers who need a degree to get promotion.

In the last few years, the number of unemployed and manual workers enrolling with the OU has gradually crept up (though never beyond 15 per cent) but the chances of attracting any more in significant numbers have been dashed by disproportionate fee rises imposed by the Conservative Government.

In other areas of adult education attempts have been made to overcome the problems associated with conventional educational formats. Alternative structures to traditional evening classes and university extra-mural courses have been set up – 'second chance' and community education projects, courses providing new opportunities for women, oral history groups, and writers' workshops.

All these initiatives are premised on the view that adult education is failing to reach a large reservoir of untapped ability and need.

Overall, adult education is in danger of becoming a middle class haven, a mecca for people who already have some education and want to take advantage of more.[2]

It is possible that Channel Four will be able to provide a combination of broadcast, written and back up materials that will engage the interests of those who'd never thought of watching an OU programme. But there will be a lot of pressures pulling the Channel's educational programming back towards already 'proven' strategies and formats. The cost of that kind of retrenchment will be that they will then fail to reach those audiences who could benefit most from what they have to offer. They could well end up reaching only those parts of the audience least in need of educational refreshment. The Annan Committee saw this hazard very clearly:

The ITCA told us that they considered that the new channel would be likely to attract advertisers aiming to reach people in the higher income groups, light ITV viewers and those whose interest in specialised programmes would be related to particular markets eg finance, industry, sport and gardening, as well as to the small advertiser, who had not been able to afford to use ITV. Their programme plans for the channel suggested to us that the service would be aimed primarily at those most able and most likely to provide themselves with other sorts of entertainment, information and education.

Further reading

The ACACE *Formal Statement & Recommendations* in response to the *White Paper on Broadcasting*, (Cmnd. 7294), ACACE November, 24, 1978.

Naomi McIntosh, 'To Make Continuing Education a Reality', *Oxford Review of Education*, Vol.5, No.2, 1979.

ACACE Report, *Continuing Education: From Policies to Practice*, ACACE, Leicester, 1982.

CHAPTER 6

Independent Television News: mutton dressed as lamb?

Barry Flynn

Given that Channel Four is committed to 'saying new things in new ways', it is perhaps surprising that responsibility for the major parts of its new output has been awarded to ITN – an organisation that has done little to change its editorial routines, newsgathering practices or bulletin structures since it began broadcasting in 1955.

At that time, it quickly attracted mass audiences with its 'new' style bulletins, capitalising on its success with the creation of *News at Ten* in 1967 – consistently its most successful programme – and *First Report* (later *News at One*) in 1972. It now employs about 700 people, 150 of them journalists, to produce its 19 weekly bulletins, and has an operating budget of some £13 million (1980 figure).

The company is financed by the ITV contractors, who, for the most part, contribute to its operating and capital expenditure in proportion to their share of the industry's advertising revenue. The companies also own all of ITN's £400,000 worth of shares, and contribute an equal amount in interest-free loans. In addition, ITN helps to run UPITN, the international news film agency it formed with the American-owned press agency UPI.

The choice of ITN for the main Channel Four news contract was, in a way, inevitable. The company had lost its application for the Breakfast Television franchise, and the pressures it exerted on the IBA for a piece of the Channel Four action were considerable. It was also in the happy position of being able to provide a relatively low budget news product by relying on the present structure of its three weekday bulletins – a built-in advantage which no independent production company was likely to match.

The new organisation set up within ITN to produce news for the Fourth Channel is therefore only theoretically 'independent', and its boss, Derrick Mercer, is responsible solely to ITN's Editor, David Nicholas. What Mercer and his news team of 'specialist' reporters and journalists will be offering the Channel Four audience is an hour-long weekday bulletin from 7 to 8 pm, except for Friday evenings when it will end at 7.30.

Those expecting innovation in these programmes are likely to be disappointed. Sadly, ITN is *not* about to change the way in which editorial decisions are made, nor the way in which its bulletins are presented. Moreover, the editorial staff (many of them drawn from ITN) are *not* about to change their notions of 'professional' expertise or 'intuitions' about 'what the audience wants'. In such circumstances it becomes distressingly easy to predict the kind of news bulletins on offer and the way in which they will be produced – in a phrase: mutton dressed as lamb.

It is true that ITN does not have many models to choose from. But would it have been too much to expect that it might attempt to evolve new structures of its own? In the event, it appears to be plumping for something along the lines of the structure of BBC's *Newsnight* programme. Thus there will be extended headlines to introduce the bulletin, followed by in-depth treatment of a few stories – rather than the rapid fire treatment of compressed front-page news items typical of its other bulletins. These stories will be linked, of course, by a presenter: either Peter Sissons or Sarah Hogg.

One problem ITN faces is how to overcome two commercial breaks instead of one. Usual practice is to give a 'taster', just before the break, to entice viewers to keep watching, and then repeat a short menu of items after it. Having to re-iterate these procedures will mean that the amount of actual hard news contained in the bulletin will be considerably less than an hour – in practice about 45 minutes – once titles are subtracted from the running time, along with the commercials.

To judge by the 'pilots' already produced, ITN is having a tough time providing even *this* much air time – not surprising in view of the fact that it often has trouble filling a half-hour bulletin. Some of the 'new' areas of coverage are also causing trouble – such as the arts, science and technology, and business. The first two of these were conspicuously absent from a survey carried out earlier this year into how ITN coverage broke down into different categories during one random week.[1]

News gathering: a predictable rhythm

Whatever the structure of the bulletins, it is safe to say that most of their contents will have been decided upon well in advance. The rhythm of the country's public events is – from ITN's point of view – an extremely predictable one. A year ahead, all the important dates of sporting events will be known, and plans sketched out for possible coverage. Such recurring dates in the political calendar as the party political conferences will be on the agenda many months ahead, as well as the major trades union meetings. In the shorter term, plans can be made well in advance for such things as forthcoming byelections, annual pay negotiations and so on.

Closer to bulletin time, so-called 'look ahead' meetings take place at ITN, (usually the day before), whose main purpose is to plan the following day's coverage. The main areas of Channel Four output will probably also be decided at these. Those involved are a select group of ITN's most senior staff – the Editor, or his Deputy, that week's Home and Foreign News Editors, the Programme Producers and their Deputies, and senior representatives of the technical staff. It is at this stage that the all important decisions are taken about the allocation of reporters and camera crews to particular stories – given the constraint that some have to be kept in reserve for stories that emerge on the day.

During these meetings, the Editor may also make policy decisions about how he thinks particular stories should be covered, or suggest what possible future areas are liable to blow up into important issues. The ITN 'look ahead' meeting is thus the central part of the editorial decision-making process. It is confidential, and excludes those who actually produce the raw material from which the bulletins are constructed: the reporters, journalists and cameramen.

On the day, then, most of the Channel Four news coverage will have been pre-determined – at least in terms of who is reporting which stories and where. The daily routine of the ITN newsroom reflects this highly-planned aspect of news gathering in the exceptionally rigid organisation of its editorial routines. As can be seen (Diagram One), the sources of 'raw' news at present (Stage One) are highly dependent on *other* news organisations – the home and foreign news agencies (such as Reuter and Press Association), the radio, the BBC and Fleet Street. There is little reason to suppose that Channel Four practice will be different in any of these respects – especially since the two news teams will be working side by side in the same building using many of the same facilities.

With the day's coverage already outlined by yesterday's 'look ahead', the first thing to happen each day will be a conference for all those involved in that evening's bulletin. This is where the provisional running order of the programme is handed round, and it is largely an occasion for the programme producer to tell his staff what stories they are going to be covering. After this (Stage Two), bulletin staff will begin to assemble the agency copy they will need in

THE DAILY EVOLUTION OF CHANNEL FOUR NEWS

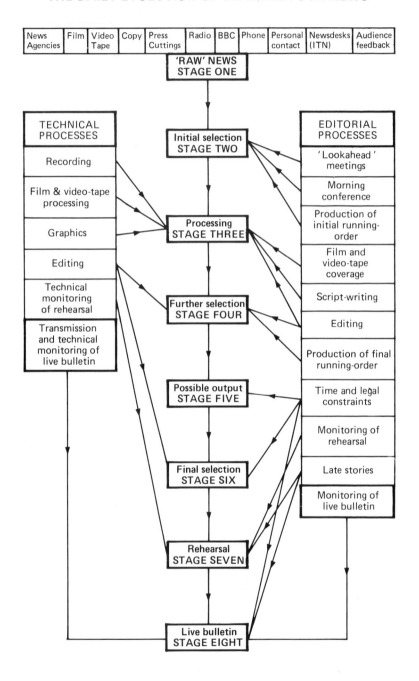

order to write the stories, view any film or video-tape available, and check up on their reporters' progress 'in the field'. They will need to be told, if necessary, of any late developments that might dictate changes in the planned treatment of their stories.

Meanwhile, filming (or in the case of video-tape, recording) has begun (Stage Three), and in some cases processing will already have started. Graphics needed for various stories are also being composed. Throughout, there is continuous interaction between the technical staff, such as film and video-tape editors, and the journalists and reporters. In many cases, the latter will already have typed out provisional scripts – sight unseen – to which the pictures will later be edited. Thus a large amount of selection and editing will be taking place 'in advance': firstly, in that large amounts of agency copy have to be compressed down to their essentials, and secondly, in that matching shots from extended sequences of film and video-tape have to be found to 'agree' with these selected fragments.

By the beginning of the afternoon, the journalists will have started passing on their first 'lead-ins' (the written introductions to reporter film packages read out by the newscaster) to a chief sub-editor, whose job is to check copy and alter it so that it is in keeping with the programme's objectives and style (Stage Four). When this has been done, it is passed on to the presenter – who also has a look at it before it is typed up and duplicated, just in case he or she should want to change anything.

By later afternoon the range of possible stories will have been processed (Stage Five) except for scheduled 'late' stories (and barring unforeseen events). Now, the programme producer's overall view of the shape of the bulletin will lead him to suggest certain 'cuts'. Since most stories are in fact written with built-in cut points in mind, this is not as problematic as it sounds. Other final decisions, such as legal ones about court cases or possible libels, are made at this point, although in principle they can be made at any time from now on.

Just before rehearsal, the final selection of items is made (Stage Six), and the ultimate cuts carried out on the available selected film and video-tape stories and scripts. The programme will still be overloaded with stories (by about 10 per cent) in case of technical problems, with well-defined priorities about which stories are to be dropped first.

During rehearsal (Stage Seven), the stories will be run through in order (even if they're not in the building yet) to make sure that the sequencing of the technical machinery is correct, and to check that the camera men and other technicians have not been asked to perform impossible tasks. Camera angles are lined up, sound and lighting levels are set, and the presenters rehearse reading through the scripts that are available to verify that the 'cueing-in' to film and video-tape 'rolls' is precise. By now, most of the editorial staff will be in the control room to watch what is going on and trouble-shoot if needed. By the time the red light goes on outside the studio to show that the bulletin is on air (Stage Eight), the electronics will largely have taken over. Any editorial decisions taken from now on will necessarily be crude.

News ideology: disorganised plagiarism

So much for what will be happening inside Channel Four's news room. But such a description conceals the assumptions and practices that underlie the procedures, many of which are highly antagonistic to any notions of 'innovative' or 'distinctly different' approaches to the news – as was said at the outset. The fact that ITN has not sought to challenge these in its new venture shows how empty its Channel Four rhetoric is.

For instance, it is clear that the convention of having a central, 'authoritative' presenter has always been one of the mainstays of broadcasters' attempts to maintain their twin fictions of 'objectivity' and 'impartiality'. The stories sent in by reporters and correspondents are all too obviously subjective views – based on an individual view of the subject matter in question – and in turn largely based on outside sources from which their perspectives on reality are culled. But with one or two high-status personalities to introduce their stories, this diversity is submerged under the implication that if, for instance, *Peter Sissons* says it is true, then the story can be trusted.

Moreover, although Channel Four news may be providing us with a slightly different range and type of story, it has not suggested a way to deal in its bulletin with what the Glasgow University Media Group termed 'inferential frameworks'. The way stories are juxtaposed, for example, adds whole ranges of implications about how the viewer is expected to interpret them. Thus, stories about crime may be slotted into the same part of the bulletin as stories about racial conflict or unemployment, or stories about pay disputes or strikes are simply strung together, regardless of their causes or the different sections of the community involved.

Nor has there been any evident attempt to challenge the visual and verbal 'grammar' of conventional television news reporting, which aids and abets these 'inferential frameworks'. The way the news treats high status and low status people re-inforces their social standing, and kowtows to social differences: the company director is interviewed in a plush office, the worker on the shopfloor. 'Ordinary' people are almost never given access to a studio, but are filmed at moments of extreme emotion and vulnerability, and rarely given the airtime any back bench MP would expect as a right. They are also given only the shortest of titles on captions when being interviewed, and in so-called (and ridiculously unrepresentative) 'vox-pops', no titles at all.

Counterpointing this treatment is a sub-tabloid commentary written in a finely-honed present tense – to give the often erroneous impression that what the viewer is watching has not only *just* happened, but happened in the first person singular to an ITN reporter. It contains a vocabulary redolent with words like 'claims' and 'alleges' that cast doubt without saying so, and in which employers 'make offers' but workers 'reject' them. It is a language in which 'I think' masquerades as 'some people would say', and in which the interviewer's questions attempt to frame the interviewee's answers.

It is in interviews, too, that the dictates of visual 'grammar' are at their most distorting. Interviews outside the studio are filmed with only one camera. Once the interview is over the camera is turned around and pointed at the reporter, who then repeats the questions (not always accurately) and smiles and nods a few times as if in reaction to what is being said. These questions and reaction shots (termed 'cutaways' and 'noddies') are then spliced into the original interview to mask the cuts that have been made in the interviewee's answers. If not, the picture would 'jump' every time a cut were made, and it would be obvious to the viewer that the answer has been altered. The 'jump-cut', as it is called, is therefore avoided at all costs, not simply because it is considered unaesthetic, but because it is a fundamental requirement of the way conventional television news programmes are produced that they should *appear totally unmediated*.

This type of obscuring of the necessarily selective processes at work in the editing of news stories is paralleled by a coyness about their origin. The major myth of ITN's news operation (and one unlikely to be challenged by the relatively small news team put together for Channel Four) is that it originates most of its own news coverage. Given ITN's heavy reliance on the ITV network for its home coverage, and on the foreign TV networks (the big American ones in particular) for its foreign news coverage, nothing could be further from the truth.

This is underlined particularly by ITN's heavy reliance on the news agencies, who determine the agenda from which ITN selects its own coverage and who supply the hard copy which, together with newspaper cuttings, forms the backbone of their bulletins. The real task for ITN journalists is the compression and rewriting of large amounts of extraneous information – not origination and investigation, which is costly and labour-intensive. But this reliance on other sources is seldom admitted, except where ITN wishes to cast doubt on the accuracy of a piece of agency information.

What is actually going on at ITN is a system of somewhat disorganised plagiarism – but it would hardly be politic for the audience to know this, especially given the organisation's 'need' to project an image of immediacy and authority. Of course, if ITN's Channel Four news operation really were a radical departure from previous norms, the priority given to such 'needs' might well be questioned.

Nevertheless, the most important hidden influence on the new ITN programmes is likely to lie with its own personnel. Since they will have been recruited only from within ITN or other mainstream broadcasting and press institutions, they will doubtless share a set of 'professional' assumptions about 'common-sense' news-values and their ability to sense 'what the public wants'. The principal logic behind this ideology – that the journalists are uniquely capable of choosing which issues and stories will most interest or affect the audience (and of ranking and treating them in equally acceptable ways) – is so lacking in foundation that in any other area of life such ideas would be regarded as convincing signs of incipient megalomania. For such a claim to be true, ITN's journalists would have to possess some highly-evolved mechanism for guaging audience interests and reactions – one which could provide a daily yardstick by which their newsvalues could be informed and altered. In fact, the only such diagnostic tool is a clumsy one: the irregular publication of ratings, which only inaccurately measure viewers' responses to bulletins-as-a-whole over a period of weeks – and not their reaction to the ordering or presentation of discrete items within a single bulletin.

Apart from hand-me-down rumours from the market research specialists as to the possible composition of a Channel Four audience, the reality of these journalistic 'intuitions' amounts merely to a complex of assumptions and prejudices fed by the journalist's own background, the views of his peers and the constraints of conforming to the consensual values of an organisation like ITN. In the end, what ITN journalists are doing is writing for each other – not for the audience. Unless some elaborate method of audience feedback is set up, Channel Four news will be produced in a vacuum according to journalistic preconceptions lifted lock, stock and barrel from the broadcasting establishment.

Diverse Production: a real 'alternative'?

Happily, there is one other company producing news on Channel Four which looks as if it may be taking on the critical and innovative initiative so manifestly lacking at ITN. Called Diverse Production, it will be responsible for a weekly half-hour of 'alternative' news on Friday nights between 7.30 and 8 pm.

The programme will be headed by David Graham – who spent six years in the 1970s working for the consumer unit of Nationwide and for Panorama – and video-artist Peter Donebauer. They and their staff (a total of 30) will be aided by a working party of contacts from different political, social and audience constituencies as well as a group of consultants that includes Greg Philo of the Glasgow University Media Group, Bruce Page, former editor of the *New Statesman* and Steve Pryle, a senior researcher at the GMWU.

Using the working party, Diverse Production plans to maintain a network of permanent 'stringer' groups – part of which will contain a cross-section of the nation's population by age, politics and socio-economic group (chosen by MORI). But they will be used neither as professional newsgatherers nor as 'representative spokesmen' for their respective communities or constituencies. Instead, they are intended to be a point of contact through which such groups can make regular contributions to mainstream television: Diverse sees itself as a TV publisher.

The format of the Friday Perspective programme is to have three items in the half-hour slot, each of which will be a topical report from the week's news, but from the viewpoint of one of the various groups. They may say, 'We saw the story but that wasn't how it seems to us,' or perhaps, 'the most important story was missed out altogether.' In addition, there will be an attempt to cover foreign news (finances permitting) and occasional items on how the other media are dealing with the news. But what seems most promising about David Graham's outfit is that he seems willing to challenge just those professional ideologies evident in conventional news bulletins which were detailed earlier in the description of ITN's Channel Four broadcasts.

For a start, there will be *no* presenter. As David Graham says: 'The programmes' avoidance of personal continuity fits with its pluralistic, non-consensual nature.' Instead, items will be linked by electronic graphics. Secondly, the network of 'stringer' groups, if successful, will bypass the agencies' agenda-setting and ensure that the news is as first hand as it can be. These groups' opinions, in fact, rather than the Diverse staff's, will form the filter through which each weekly programme is focussed. There will therefore not only be a proper 'audience feedback' system to ensure that it is opinions in the world outside that determine news values, but representatives of the public will, for once, be exerting a real influence on programme content.

The danger is that the 'stringer' groups themselves will still be so heavily influenced by established traditions of 'news values' that they will be doing the agencies' agenda-setting for them. Nevertheless, the problem of how to determine news values will have been defined: it will not be what Friday Perspective's journalists *think* the audience wants from the news, but in some measure what the audience *says* it wants.

David Graham is also known to be sympathetic to attempts to change the visual and verbal 'grammar' that so subtly delivers its political messages through the journalistic conventions of film and copy editing. Obviously, the critique of ITN practice made earlier carries within it the seeds for any suggested remedies. A striking trades unionist might, for instance, be interviewed in the environment of his own home, instead of in his customary place on a picket line outside the factory gates. More radically, he might be ignored altogether in favour of an 'alternative' perspective that occasionally viewed the *employer* as the 'problem-causer' rather than the trades unions. Zooming in to catch every twitch of emotion on a bereaved women's face might be ended in favour of introducing similar close-ups of members of the establishment whilst under questioning. Why not allow members of the public to address the camera directly on occasion – instead of insisting that what they have to say should be aimed obliquely at an interviewer?

As for changing the verbal 'grammar', a simple rule book could be drawn up listing words or practices to be avoided. Newspapers have books of 'house style' – why not a news programme? Such innovations, painstaking though they might be, might mean that the artifice that all journalists take for granted in the production of apparently unmediated news would be laid bare, and, if necessary, destroyed.

It is this radical burden that will prove most difficult for Diverse to discharge. For it demands nothing less than that its staff impose a continual self-consciousness on their work until new editorial routines have been established. It will mean braving the IBA Charter's requirements for 'due impartiality' by making it clear that every news progamme, 'alternative' or otherwise, is a collection of highly subjective personal perspectives, and could not be otherwise.

If genuine attempts are made to carry through such a radical reshaping of broadcast news conventions, it will entail a constant debate among its practitioners that will be difficult to pursue under the weight of programme deadlines. Moreover, it may well produce results which will evoke at least initial antagonism from many quarters – not least from an audience grown accustomed to the products of the 'spectacular' 'news-as-entertainment' industry.

But for all the immense difficulties that face Friday Perspective – and although it might be tempting to dismiss its 'alternative' outlook as mere tokenism on the part of its Channel Four masters – it promises to be a worthwhile experiment which will repay careful viewing.

CHAPTER 7

Women command the flagship?

Lesley Hilton

'Channel Four's weekly half-hour current affairs programme will address the same audience as *Panorama* and *World in Action*, but will differ in at least two ways. Its peaktime slot will certainly *not* be on Mondays, when those two programmes currently compete... Secondly, while men will not be excluded from working on the programmes, women will make all the editorial decisions. They will not be tackling purely women's subjects, nor addressing a female audience. The idea, according to Liz Forgan, "has nothing to do with positive discrimination or social justice. It is a *journalistic* experiment. Given that roughly half the world is female and given that the vast majority of the editorial decisions in newspapers, radio and TV are taken by men, there seems to us a glimmer of a chance that we, the media, may not always be getting the story right."'

Channel Four Press Release, April 1982.

'I hope that I am wrong in gleaning from your questions a very strong feeling that you are less interested in the success of these programmes than in catching me out in some failure of proper feminist orthodoxy or in fighting out personal arguments over who got commissions and why or why not. I do believe that the people directly involved have put that stuff behind them in a determination to get on with what is much more important – making this current affairs series a triumphant success in what we both know will be the teeth of every kind of criticism, ridicule and carping from the world at large. If people like you are going to be picking away at the foundations from the other side of the wall it is going to be even more tough.'

From a letter from Liz Forgan, Senior Commissioning Editor for Actuality, Channel Four, replying to my request for information, June 1982.

Made by men, for men . . .

The original idea for such a programme came from the Women's Broadcasting and Film Lobby, set up in 1979 to improve the employment and training opportunities for women in the film and television industry and to challenge sexist and stereotyped images of women appearing in the media. In November 1979 members of WBFL had a meeting with the IBA at which they explained their concern over the position of women within the television industry:

'We repeated that women are 51% of the population and generally the majority of the viewing audience, even for current affairs. Yet most programmes are made by men, from a male viewpoint, with a male viewer in mind, which limits the subjects covered and leads to the portrayal of women in stereotyped ways. There is a tendency to divide subjects into 'general' issues and 'women's' issues – there don't seem to be men's issues. If a current affairs programme covers a 'woman's' issue, it is considered to have 'done' women – you won't get a programme about childminders within three months, or maybe much longer, or one on abortion, despite the fact that they are obviously very different issues. A subject seen as a 'woman's' issue is lucky to get an airing at all in prime time – it is quite likely to be dismissed as more suitable for afternoon programmes. The IBA should actively encourage a different attitude on the fourth channel.' (From the WBFL minutes of the meeting with the IBA.)

Although many women work in television, only 1% of them are producers and directors and most of those are in the so-called women's areas of education, drama and children's programmes. The main TV union, the Association of Cinematograph, Television and Allied Technicians (ACTT), published a report in 1975 called 'Patterns of Discrimination', but no real steps were taken to improve opportunities for women in the industry until the appointment of the ACTT's first Equality Officer in 1982.

During the Women's Session at the 1980 Edinburgh Television Festival, chaired by Anna Ford, the idea of a programme made by women was taken up by several people present. For example, Mary Holland said 'that the gross imbalance in employment, especially at the top, means that programme content is determined by men. Women's news is simply not regarded as news by those who guard the news values and decide on content. When did you last – or when did you ever – see serious coverage on TV of what has happened in the women's movement?' Jeremy Isaacs took up the idea of equality for women in television production in an interview with Liz Forgan, then Women's Editor of *The Guardian*, at the end of that year – and when she joined Channel Four (as Senior Commissioning Editor for Actuality) the plans were hatched although to quote from an article written by her for *Cosmopolitan* magazine in March 1982: 'Several critics said they could not see the point; either it would be a good current affairs programme, in whch case it would be just like all the other good current affairs programmes, or it would be bad and demonstrate the incompetence of women in serious things...'

One of the first things that she did in her new job was to give a grant of £15,000 to a group of women called Broadside to run an advisory service for women working (or wanting to work) in television. Broadside also drew up a list of advisors – women from many areas who could either contribute programme ideas or could help other women to realise those ideas on film. Many of the members of Broadside are also in WBFL and include producers, directors, researchers, journalists, academics and technicians. They all have a strong committment to the idea of equality of opportunity for women in television production.

Questions of control

There have been one or two changes of direction in Liz Forgan's plans for the slot. Her original premise was that it would be a programme produced by women; it is now a programme where the major editorial decisions are taken by women. She still maintains that there is no difference that 'the governing intelligence – the eyes, choice and instinctive minds – must be female.' In the *Cosmopolitan* article mentioned earlier she wrote: 'I don't know what sort of current affairs programme will emerge from an editorial group of women... Different stories might be thought important; familiar stories might be tackled from a different angle; different witnesses might be called or the same witnesses might speak differently when talking to a woman... I don't believe that women are the same as men or that they see the world in the same way (although they can quickly be trained to do so) but we are missing that female perspective from a whole strand of what is called serious journalism. It is not a matter of paying attention only to subjects that interest women. What is missing is an instinctive response towards what is important and what isn't; what is serious and what is frivolous; which tone of voice commands attention and which doesn't. There is only one way to put that dimension back into the picture of the world which we see on our screens or find in our papers, and that is to have women as well as men making the mainstream editorial choices... It is not a matter of making special allowances for the poor dears and letting them drone on about their preoccupations while the rest of the audience tunes into something else. The fact is that we are wasting women's eyes and ears and brains and wits by putting all kinds of filters between them and the media of communication. Take away some of those filters – traditional employment and promotional patterns, male-dominated editorial choices and attitudes – and there is a good chance of some fresh water flowing into the main stream.'

A slight hiccup occurred over the actual allocation of the contracts. Liz Forgan had originally thought of giving as many groups as possible short runs of programmes, but gradually realised that was impracticable because 'a) it made the cost prohibitive and b) it did not give anyone long enough to get their feet on the ground, make their mistakes and come right in the end.' She then decided to award 40 programmes to one company, but the Channel Four board rejected that idea on the grounds that it could lead to mere slot-filling. The final result was the allocation of 31 programmes to one company and 16 to another. The two successful companies are Gambles Milne and Broadside. Ten groups put in applications altogether and there was a lot of manoeuvering and regrouping before the final contracts were announced. Several names appeared on more than one application!

Gambles Milne (31 programmes) is headed by Lyn Gambles and Claudia Milne. They have never worked together before but both are experienced in television production. Lyn Gambles started as a Reuters journalist and has been a researcher and director at Thames. She produced 'The Risk Business' for the BBC and has worked on many other projects. Claudia Milne has worked on World in Action, among other things, and was a founder member of the ACTT Equality Committee. They will be joint executive producers with a staff of about 20.

The company's plans are for single topic shows which 'explore ways out of problems' and 'find new perspectives on current stories.' Gambles and Milne say they want to present the show 'in an up to the minute way' although they 'do not want to be enslaved by new technology.' They also say that they want to foster the use of more women in technical grades and that although they expect their production team to be composed mainly of women they stress that they do not have a separatist policy towards men. To quote from their proposal to Channel Four: 'As executive producers we intend to have full discussions with the production team ... While this team has an unashamedly hierarchical structure, our experience of current affairs tells us that decisions have to be taken quickly. There is just not time for consultation.'

Broadside (16 programmes) intends to be a less hierarchical organisation with 12 company directors, one of whom is Dianne Tammes (the first woman in England to get an ACTT camera ticket.) They will have a production team of ten with freelances brought in when needed. They have a clear commitment to using women technicians and also to trying to involve the crews in the editorial process, by bringing them in to help set up the programmes rather than just hiring at the last minute. Whether or not the unions will allow a more collective way of working remains to be seen.

Broadside will also be doing single topic shows from a woman's perspective. For example, from the existing media you would think that unemployment was a purely male problem. Or, another possible example given me by Broadside's Helen Baehr, how the cuts in the welfare state have lead to more 'community care' – that is, unpaid female labour. Broadside intend to show how their stories are constructed and where their information comes from; they feel it is important to stress to viewers that what appears as news and current affairs in the media are only other peoples' selective opinions of what is important. So, for example, they might say at the start of a programme 'these are the stories that the news media focused' on this week. Out of these we have chosen/have not chosen/are looking at a new aspect of . . . ' They think that they should also explain why certain people were or were not selected to be interviewed, for example on the basis of availability/ability to talk/relevance etc. This would serve to remind viewers that all editorial decisions are subjective.

Broadside's original proposal to Channel Four included their involvement in the channel's news output, but the awarding of the contract to ITN has ruled that out. They have some reservations about the singling out of a slot for women, thus possibly creating another ghetto area, and hope that Channel Four will adopt a positive action policy towards women in *all* its commissioned productions. They feel it is important that the Channel's output is constantly challenged and is not allowed to remain as male-dominated as the other three channels.

One of the groups who failed to win a contract was Battle Axe – half a dozen women based around the magazine *Spare Rib*. They were probably the most radically feminist group that applied and they feel that they didn't get anywhere because of this. (In an interview with Elizabeth Garrett published in the *Daily Express*, July 2, 1982, Liz Forgan gave her own view of feminism: 'Modern feminism takes the view that, though women are in every way equal human beings with men, we are not at all the same creatures. We shouldn't strive to be *like* men, and behave in butch ways, but become surer of ourselves, and trust our own natural instincts. It is this confident, non-strident female voice that Channel Four is committed to encourage.')

Battle Axe's first submission was for a series of standard current affairs subjects looked at from a feminist viewpoint. They wanted to be able to respond to the news of the week and gave two examples: 1) Hiroshima Day and how women in Japan felt about it now/the neutron bomb and Reagan's policies/the fact that the defence establishment is still entirely male-dominated, and 2) Toxteth – how the women in the area felt about their kids being out on the streets. When they realised there wasn't enough money available to do quick response programmes Battle Axe changed their application to straight documentaries on subjects like sex education, schools and law and order tackled from a hardline feminist perspective. When that didn't seem to be getting anywhere they ended up submitting two documentary ideas – one on the history of the women's liberation movement and the other on sexuality. Liz Forgan says that these ideas were not dropped because of their radical feminism, but Battle Axe told me: 'We were set up to be used as the expendable extreme element. We felt that Liz Forgan was too inexperienced to handle the situation properly and she set up a "consultative" situation and built us in as the ones to jettison.'

At least one other group of women considered applying for a contract but decided against on the grounds that the budget was too low to allow the programmes to be done properly. The budget per programme is £30,000 (above and below-the-line costs) to be paid in a lump sum for all the programmes together. This is said to allow for the fact that some will cost more than others to make, so the money can be juggled accordingly. But for a comparable programme like World in Action the figure of £30,000 would probably just about cover the above-the-line costs *only* on a domestic story (below-the-line costs of crewing, administration, offices etc are already paid for by the company).

In a way the awarding of two contracts has set up a competitive situation although Liz Forgan says that she doesn't see the two companies as competitors. 'They are two excellent groups of talented and professional women but they are not in a race – although they might look over their shoulders from time to time,' she said. Eleanor Stephens, Broadside's editor, responded to that as follows: 'Although the scheduling presents problems of competitiveness, we intend to make sure that there is co-operation and goodwill. As far as the viewers are concerned it is one slot. If one production company fails the other one will suffer too.'

Putting on a good show

So much for the history. But why should Liz Forgan be so defensive about her plans, as the letter quoted at the beginning suggests. Could it be that despite all the brave talk from Channel Four about their commitment to 'new ideas/new programmes/new faces' they have found themsleves in a Catch 22 situation? Liz Forgan has felt the pressure to put on a good show (literally) and in television terms that doesn't necessarily have anything to do with innovative ideas; it often has more to do with slick (uncontroversial) presentation. So, if you're a Commissioning Editor faced with those pressures do you take the risk of using inexperienced people with bright ideas who might forget to take the lens cap off the camera, or do you go for proven professionals who you know will at least get the thing on the screen the right way up, but who will probably go on making the same old television that they always have?

Liz Forgan says she is calling the series 'a journalistic experiment' to stop people calling it a social experiment. She emphasises it is not an exercise in positive discrimination and that well qualified men have not been rejected in favour of less well qualified women. To quote again from the article in the *Daily Express*: 'The hope is that the new, all female teams will demonstrate that something very significant is often missing from the news. Then, gradually, after the point has been made and established, some men might be allowed in as well.' It would appear that while she may not have discriminated against men, she has discriminated against non-professional women. For example, Gambles and Milne are proven pros in their field who can be trusted to provide *something* even if it is a World in Action copy. Their advertisement for production staff to work on their programmes asks for applicants who 'possess relevant experience and qualifications for the post.' Surely almost by definition anyone possessing 'relevant experience and qualifications' is going to have spent several years working for another broadcast television company and so will be steeped in the traditions of television. Someone like that may well be short on truely innovative ideas for a new sort of current affairs and in a tight spot will almost certainly fall back on well tried TV practice, rather than *really* having to innovate. So, if the channel is privileging 'professionals', where are the new ideas and new forms of television going to come from?

The ITV companies themselves have to some extent been caught napping by the creation of this current affairs series. At the end of last year Thames TV held a series of meetings for women in the company to suggest ideas that could be put forward for this slot. Bearing this in mind, I asked Liz Forgan two pertinent questions:

Q. *When these contracts end are Thames, or any other ITV com-panies, serious contenders for the next year?*

A. Next year, as this year, any individual or group or company is free to submit proposals and we shall choose the best one or ones.

Q. *If they are, won't this undermine the spirit of the enterprise because they would a) be jumping on the bandwagon, b) be able to undercut the independents and c) although they may set up women's production units, the hierarchy of their man-agement is male dominated anyway?*

A. We are really at cross purposes I am afraid and the tone of this question demonstrates it. This is not a reward for struggle or a cricket match to be played by some rules of good behaviour. If some other group which never thought for a minute of making TV programmes, or women making current affairs pro-grammes, until they see our screens next year, suddenly decide to 'jump on the bandwagon' I am afraid that my only concern will be how good I think their programmes are likely to prove. Of course a lot of considerations go into that 'good' but I flatly refuse to accept that some groups have special right of access just because they have done the spade work in the women's movement. That earns them my respect, my admira-tion, possibly even a generous measure of the benefit of the doubt should that arise, but it does not give them some pre-emptive right to have programmes commissioned by Channel Four.

The question of undercutting the independents has been dealt with at huge length elsewhere. The answer is that inde-pendents can almost always make programmes cheaper than the ITCA companies and though the companies can some-times do package deals with us, if you look at the way the balance of commissioning is working out this year you cannot possibly say the independents are being put at a disadvantage. The answer to c) is that if the fact that Thames management is predominantly male interferes with the exercise of editorial control by women, then that would make them ineligible for this slot.

Obviously as a woman working in television I wish this slot the very best of luck, but I don't think we should all rush to our televi-sion sets in November expecting to see anything startlingly differ-ent. All the women involved in this programme (with the exception of Liz Forgan, who has no previous TV experience) have been around broadcast television for a while and the conventions of televi-sion take a long time to unlearn – and they will have to be unlearned before alternatives can present themselves. It will take a while before the production teams can come up with anything really new, and it may take longer than the year that the contracts last. If that is the case it would be a shame if the programmes were to be judged too soon — they must be given time to develop. Many people will be wanting them to fail — or at least not to succeed. Women only need to make one mistake for people to say, 'Told you they couldn't do it.' It is very important that this slot is seen as a means to an end and not as an end in itself. It should serve as a jumping-off point for programme and staffing policies throughout the television industry which would make the need for a women's 'protected slot' unnecessary.

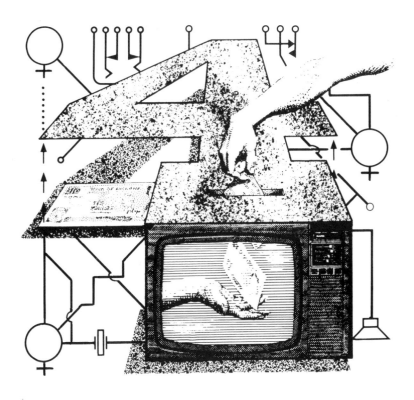

Programming
for/by women

The arrival of the new channel has been notable for a series of statements by its Chief Executive, Jeremy Isaacs, indicating an awareness that the new channel would not easily be allowed to reproduce
the traditional structures of exclusion of women from positions of
power in broadcasting. This awareness can perhaps be seen in his
early appointment – in January 1981 – of Liz Forgan and Naomi
Mackintosh as two of the channel's three Senior Commissioning
Editors.

The contribution here from the Women's Advisory and Referral
Service Action Group questions the extent of the channel's commitment to greater participation by women in programme-making, and
argues for the appointment of a Commissioning Editor for Women.

CHAPTER 8

Opportunity knocks (but not very hard)

Women's Advisory and Referral Service Action Group

It is remarkable that although the television industry is no more than three decades old, most women have been as effectively shut out from any real participation as if the industry had begun three centuries ago. With the advent of a new channel the opportunity emerges for redefining women's role in television. The implications of Channel Four's initial brief and its public statements led women who were regarding the industry critically to expect that here was potential for change. 'Channel Four wants programmes that show women as they are and as they would be rather than as they have been thought to be and according to them, forced to be'

— Jeremy Isaacs, *Broadcast* July 3, 1982

Beyond verbal commitments

It is the gap between verbal commitment and practical commitment that the Women's Advisory and Referral Service wants to close. Although Channel Four as a commissioning body has instigated a more open structure for access to air-time they appear to be demanding that would be programme makers have proven expertise and strong financial backing.

The view of our group is that it is not enough to open the door and assume that those who have been excluded up to now will be in a position to come forward and take up new opportunities. A few women are being given opportunities by the new channel, but most women have as little access to Channel Four as they have to the other broadcasting institutions. In this sense Channel Four merely reproduces the structure of exclusion of women prevalent throughout the industry.

Soon after its inception Channel Four took an initiative which they hoped would go some way to combatting these problems. Following a proposal from Broadside, (an all women production company), Channel Four allocated a budget of £15,000 for a six month period. The original brief from Liz Forgan included the following statement:

The purpose of this budget is really to get Broadside established as an umbrella organisation for developing and packaging a range of programmes predominantely contributed by women. *Red Flannel*

Broadside proceeded to contact and advise women who were potential programme makers and contributors to the new channel, but who lacked the necessary expertise or knowledge to put forward their proposals. There was a huge response and many of the enquiries were beyond the scope of the brief and of the funding Broadside had received.

By the time the funding ran out in March 1982, it had become very clear that there was an acute need to continue and expand the Advisory Service. Broadside's increased activities as a Production Company meant that they no longer felt able to administer the Advisory Service. A group of women from the IFA and ACTT amongst others got together to discuss how to consolidate this initiative.

An open meeting was called for February 27, 1982 in order that the whole issue could be discussed with as many women as possible. Over 200 women attended representing film and video workshops both regional and London based, independent film makers, all the media unions, women working within the film and television industry and women's groups not yet involved in the media.

It was felt that the shape of the Advisory Service should now change. It was essential for it to operate independently of any production company, and with a more representative and broader based membership.

It was also felt that the scope of the Advisory Service should be widened: rather than providing and packaging a range of programmes for Channel Four, it was felt that it should provide a springboard to enable women to submit their own programme proposals whether as groups or individuals. There was also a strong demand, from the meeting, that Channel Four be held to its declaration of support for greater participation by women in programme-making. The continued funding of an Advisory Service was seen as crucial to this, and an Action Committee was set up to approach Channel Four for funding.

Access, information, training

In preparation for applying to Channel Four the Action Committee discussed and formulated a draft of aims for the Women's Advisory Referral Service. The basic assumption is that we should be informed by the demands of the Women's Liberation Movement and that our purpose is to encourage positive images of women in the media.

At the core of women's exclusion from broadcasting are the issues of access to information and training. Firstly, in order to provide information we plan to run a non-profit making advisory and referral service, and to produce a regularly updated folder of information and contacts covering all aspects of film, television and video production. It is important for women to have information on such things as script presentation, comparative laboratory costs and conditions, procedures in hiring performers and musicians, problems in location shooting etc. This kind of information must be easily available to all women who want to be involved in programme making. Secondly, we would press for and publicise training schemes in which women can learn the necessary skills. The informal networks that have grown up over the last ten years as women have started to trickle into the industry have been invaluable. Recognising the vital need for women to share information and contacts, we would aim to expand and maintain a national and international network of women working in the media.

The Action Group envisages the Advisory Service being run from an office in London and from a regional office, staffed by at least two paid workers, and that research work would be commissioned on a free-lance basis. We feel that it is especially important to reach out to groups of women who have not previously had a voice in the media. During the Action Group's period of activity and lobbying, we have received a great deal of interest and written support for the project. The Advisory Service has been formally mentioned at various events including 'The Guardian Lecture', 'Sexism in the Media' Conference and 'Talking Shop' held at Watershed. The recent 'Women Live' month initiated by Women In Entertainment has given us the opportunity to inform women of our aims at a wide range of events. Although lack of resources means we are unable to operate the information service in any formal way as yet, many individual members are being asked for the sort of information and advise the service will provide. Questions range from: Where can I find out information about budgeting, forming a company, equipment hire, contracts, etc? to requests for names of women technicians available to work on women's films.

Since their initial support of the Advisory Service run by Broadside, there has been little evidence of Channel Four's active commitment to a greater participation by women. There are a number of indications which lead to a suspicion that Channel Four's verbal commitment may not be concretely realised. In Channel Four's recent publicity booklet, there is little reference made to women. We feel that Channel Four should have a positive policy about women and be prepared to publish it and act upon it.

As Channel Four commissions programmes from production companies rather than making programmes themselves they can avoid establishing a positive policy towards the employment of women on the programmes they fund. In examining programme – proposals are they asking for a percentage of women to be included in all production crews, not just on 'women's' programmes? Are they going to encourage and instigate training schemes for women technicians? Where are the commissions for women to produce drama, prestigious documentaries, sport, light entertainment? In each case the answer is very discouraging.

Putting women in control?

The fact that women are not, with a very few exceptions, being commissioned in traditionally male controlled areas of television is bad enough and evidence that nothing much is changing at Channel Four. But what is outrageous is that Channel Four is allowing Production Companies with self-styled 'feminist' male producers to co-opt feminist ideas; thus fulfilling Channel Four's alleged interest in these subjects while not putting them into the hands of women to produce. Already we have heard of major historical documentary series on Women's History and Early Feminists which have been given to male producers with no guarantee that they will use women directors or technicians. In fact some of the programmes are already earmarked for male writers and directors. Furthermore women putting forward proposals in these areas are being told that the subjects are already being covered. A programme on 'Birth/Abortion?' is being made by a male 'expert' in the subject as if men's control of Childbirth and Gynaecology hadn't gone on long enough. Programmes directed by men however 'well intentioned' will obviously never reflect a woman's point of view. Once again, on an 'innovative' Channel, our ideas and lives are to be presented by men arrogant enough to assume that they can interpret for us. As long as it is seen as acceptable for men to make programmes co-opting women's ideas, women are going to be restrained from gaining the experience to produce and be in control of their own material.

Women need to gain control over the production of television so they can make programmes which show women in their own right rather than as playing passive roles as wives, mothers, daughters, prostitutes or as victims of male violence. Television companies must make a positive effort to show women's capacity to be in control of their own lives, without excluding the obstacles women face.

Although there is an encouragingly high proportion of women commissioning editors in Channel Four, there is no one whose sole job it is to look after the interests of women programme-makers and viewers. Both ethnic minorities and young people have their own commissioning editors. We feel that unless one person in Channel Four has overall responsibility for promoting a more radical and dynamic image of women on television, women will be neglected by default. It can never be assumed that women's interests will be automatically taken care of.

We are aware of the danger of isolating programmes made by women into a 'ghetto' slot. This is far from our intention. Although some programmes put forward by women could be financed by a Commissioning Editor for women her role should be to actively encourage funding for programmes made by women across the whole range of the channel's output. We feel that it is also essential that this Commissioning Editor for Women should go out and actively seek proposals, especially from amongst sections of the community who may be unaware of the possibilities available.

A Commissioning Editor for Women could and should ensure that the door is not closed before women have time to submit proposals, as is now happening. Channel Four must recognise that people who have not had access to television training and experience up until now cannot be expected to respond as quickly to the new opportunities opened up by the channel as those who are the privileged possessors of production companies and proven track records.

So far Channel Four has not appointed a Commissioning Editor for Women. Whether this post is created or not there remains a crucial need for an advisory and referral service. Women need an external source of information about programme making on all levels and to find networks of support and encouragement. An advisory service run by women for women must go a long way towards breaking through the wall of male exclusion many women face in the film and television industry. Women in the Action Group already represent a wide variety of women's groups and organisations with an interest in changing the position of women in the media. As yet there is nowhere that women across the whole spectrum of film and video practise can share information and skills. We feel that such a pool of skill and knowledge could be a powerful means of breaking down isolation and giving women a sense of working together for radical change in the film and television industry.

The opportunities for change opened up by Channel Four should not be lost through neglect. It is important that future generations of women are in a position to make full and representative contribution to British Television. This will not happen unless positive steps are taken to remedy the effects of past discrimination. Unless Channel Four takes decisive steps in the direction we are advocating they will fail women, they will fail themselves, and they will fail the viewing public at large. They will have no grounds to consider themselves truely committed to 'innovative television'.

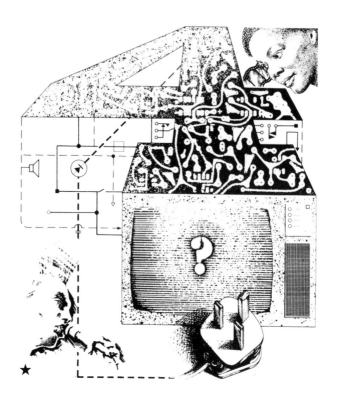

Channel Four
and youth

Young people are a prime object for the attention of broadcasters –
from 'Teddyboys' to 'Punks' to 'Rioters', youth has provided TV
with news. Youth is clearly good copy. Here, however, Youth TV
spell out the need for young people to be subject rather than object
in broadcasting – to be able to make their own programmes, speaking with their own voices and images, rather than always being
spoken about. The group set out their criticisms of mainstream
broadcasting, and go on to outline their plans for future work.

CHAPTER 9

Pushing through the screen

Youth TV

You can only take so much insult and condescension. In October 1980, we decided to take on the youth stereotypes and play the Media at their own game. We created Youth Television.

We focused on television because its bias is more insidious than that of radio or newspapers. The small box is part of the family, the news seems terribly reasonable, objective and unconfused; unquestionable. The prejudices that are the stock of light entertainment and the made-for-television movies are unchallenged. The status quo is displayed in glorious technicolour.

Youth TV aimed to challenge the media's images of youth; to force the media to take account of young people's views; to persuade the television companies to broadcast programmes about, rather than just catering for, young people, and to let them be involved in the making of those programmes.

The media speaks in images – conjured up by strident headlines videoed visions and crackling voices. There is no time to look too closely. A new war, a new strike, a new hairstyle. It's all new, so it's all news. For our easy digestion, to ease the public's consumption, all our thoughts are pre-packaged into nice little bundles: good, bad, white, black, traditional, modern, MEN, female sport, politics, SEX, love ... divide, label, segregate ... PRODUCT.

And what is the latest product?

It's 'Youth! The World Cup had its rampaging yobs. The Falklands had its brave young men – the same ones who would have been the lazy doleboys or the pitiful statistics of youth unemployment had they not been sent to war.

It is reassuring in this uncertain world to know that being young we are so easy to understand. We are the Threatened or the Threatening, an exaggerated caricature, not people. Either we are dangerous youths, irresponsible vandals in search of destructive pleasure or subversive fanatics, infiltrating political parties – or we are mindless sponges, impressionable young persons in danger of being brainwashed by left-wing extremists and, just occasionally, fascists.

We are not naive. Growing up in 1982 has a crushing effect on innocence. Young people are not all idealistic. A lot are so disillusioned they don't care anymore; if anything that is where the violence comes from. When young people do show that they have ideals, and are prepared to act on them, then they should be helped.

Making a start

We started by attending an Independent Broadcasting Authority public meeting to discuss the performance of the ITV companies and the proposals for a fourth channel. After making a brief speech from the floor we were swamped by TV producers. To our amazement, instead of angry denials and sawed-off tripods, they brandished offers of 'access' to their programmes: 'You're just what we've been looking for.'

We were pleased, but wary of the motives. In the next few weeks Youth TV evolved into a group of 25 people from across London. At first it was complete chaos: 20 people crammed into someone's bedroom, all talking at once, trying to develop a plan of action. Slowly we learnt how to work together, how to be efficient and still give everyone a say. Some people left and others came. Those that had the time and the commitment took on the responsibilities of coordinating the group, leaving others free to finish exams or be involved in specific projects. Now in 1982, there are about 20 members, with four of us forming the active nucleus. Theo Turner, Samantha Taylor, Zadoc Nava and Peter Best.

Our first project was to make a series for Thames TV's five-minute *Help* programme. We decided on two minutes of it for the 'Schools against the Bomb' campaign. The group described its origins with a viewing of the banned BBC documentary *The War Game*, and outlined its campaign to get the BBC to broadcast it.

Thames decided to ban the programme too. They said it was not impartial. It obviously lacked that elusive balance.

We managed to get quite a lot of publicity about the banning of the *Help* programme. Consequently we were invited onto two of the 'youth programmes' that had been sprouting up like daisies since the autumn of 1980.

Check It Out in Newcastle for Tyne-Tees TV was great; they gave us the time and freedom to state our case. The second, *Oxford Road Show* was a shining example of what is wrong with youth programmes. We made a brief presentation to the studio audience, and then opened up a discussion. After about three minutes it was starting to get interesting, someone asked us what we thought of the

Oxford Road Show and guess what? they cut to a band. Like *White* ('the genuine voice of youth') *Light* and most of the other youth programmes, it is assumed that young people cannot concentrate on anything serious for more than a few minutes. So a rock band or dance troupe is thrown in, between earnest features on unemployment, and a slightly spiky-haired producer speaking through his lunch.

Something Else (BBC-2) was the original youth programme. It is the best, because it is made by young people, each programme by a different group in a different part of the country. This is unique, but creates its own problems: each group, having only one chance, tries to cram in too much. When we made a *Something Else*, we tried to avoid this, by concentrating on one subject: divorce from the young people's point of view.

The events that followed its completion in June drowned its significance when it was finally broadcast in September. If 'youth' still needed a vehicle to push them to the forefront of Media coverage, then the summer riots provided it: 'Youths run Riot' . . . 'Punish Parents For Their Looting Children' . . . 'The Young Petrol Bomber' . . . 'Extremists Are Arming Our Young'.

It did achieve something. It convinced the television companies of the need to give young people the opportunity to voice their views and dissatisfactions.

There is now a plethora of programmes catering for youth. Some *have* avoided the fast-and-furious format. Programmes like *20th Century Box* treat us with some respect, instead of assuming we are morons.

After a year of activity we had done the rounds of 'access-slots' Access is a pressure valve: discontented pressure groups are allowed to let off steam. The token is thrown on the table as proof of the wide variety of views presented on television, and the industry's openness to criticism. We would like to believe that our access slots had contributed to the changing attitude towards young people, but we're afraid that the commercial considerations of recouping the lost youth audience were far more convincing arguments.

New images of youth

By 1981, Channel Four was becoming a reality. It was committed to providing more programmes for young people and to encouraging innovation. We approached Mike Bolland, the creator of *Something Else*, with proposals for a series. Since then we have been commissioned to do the research and scripting for two of these ideas,

'Images of Youth' and 'A Sketch For Someone' and have set up a production company: the Youth Broadcasting Company.

Images of Youth is about the way in which the media portrays young people and how it contrasts with the way young people see themselves. For example we will be looking at the various coverage of skinheads, and at various other youth cults and tribes – not in the typical 'shock-horror' coverage of the media but about the truth, why people feel the need to belong to such tribes, and how violent they really are. We will also be looking at the pressures exerted on young girls, and.how they are influenced by 'Teenage Magazines'. Throughout the programme we will be examining the positive attributes of young people and their actions and how these are rarely covered by the Press or television. Hopefully such a programme will make people think before condemning all young people alike as either aggressive young hooligans or vulnerable, easily manipulated idealists, and this is an important point about both programmes, that they are to be made for all generations, not only other young people. Instead of adopting a traditional documentary approach we want a more dramatic style, a mixture of vitriol and wit, satirical speechs and ludicrous (though not uncommon) attitudes, sketches and interviews. These different styles need to be carefully interchanged to produce a full and more positive image of youth; not the confusion of most youth programmes.

'A Sketch For Someone' will be different, it is far more like drama than documentary, and looks at the way people are isolated from one another – at home, at school on the dole, at work, in old age. The script deals with three main characters, each at a different age and deals with each's feelings of isolation, using poetry, songs, music, photographs and film.

We also plan a series of real access programmes. Instead of young people being put into a strange studio and asked to state their views in 39 seconds, or planned programmes involving technology they are not allowed to operate, we would broadcast videos they had made themselves on U-matic equipment which is available in their local communities, or which we could provide.

Our experiences with Mike Bolland show that he is prepared to take a risk and involve young people at production level; a policy we feel is essential to produce accurate and pertinent programmes for youth. Without such involvement it is almost inevitable that youth programmes will appear patronising or facile, how can someone who is not young really understand what people of this generation are really concerned with. Of course this is a generalisation, but the evidence exists to support this view. Youth programmes have been unsatisfactory, it is time to give young people a voice and a chance to prove themselves.

To continue our pressure group activities we have been setting up a Youth Communications Network. During the past two years we have received hundreds of letters from young people supporting our efforts and wanting to do something themselves. We are helping them to set up groups in their own areas, by linking up local youth theatre groups, youth clubs, fanzines etc, and individuals, to campaign for access to their local media. The response and enthusiasm we have found proves that not only are young people taking positive action, but that many feel the need for a voice in the media.

The first group set up outside London, in Jersey, has already had great success. They have achieved their aim of getting local discos and clubs to hold regular non-bar nights so that under 18s can be admitted. They run a thriving fanzine and are now making a one-hour programme for BBC Radio Jersey, to be a pilot for a regular Saturday show! In Liverpool several meetings have already been held, and groups in other cities are beginning to get organised. A Network of such groups would be too loud a voice to ignore.

Each group is autonomous, linked to the other groups through the network. As well as regular correspondence, a newsletter will keep everyone informed of each others activities, any nationally coordinated activities (like a festival), and act as forum for debate.

This means that what the members of the Network want to see on the television will actually be listened to and acted upon. More and more young people will be able to influence the programmes directed towards them. We hope Channel Four is ready to deal with this movement of young people standing up for themselves.

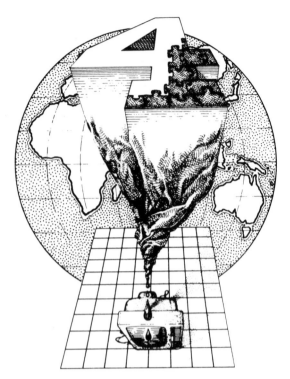

Racism, imperialism, development

It must be remembered that the Broadcasting Act 1981 has been part of the same legislative programme as the new Nationality Act. Britain has always been, de facto, defined in terms of white England: the new legislation now draws the lines of demarcation and exclusion more firmly.

Amon Saba Saakana explores in some detail the damaging consequences of the discriminatory policies and practices which Channel Four has inherited from the established world of television. He argues that the black community remains almost completely excluded from access to the new channel, and that its reliance on the 'tried and trusted' – and, you guessed it, *white* – production companies for its programmes is a form of racism-by-default, is not by intention.

Ann Zammit and Richard Bourne focus on the coverage of Third World and 'Development' issues on British television. The problems here concern how effectively the new channel will redress the neglect of the Third World in mainstream broadcasting, and how far its initiatives in this area will be ones which go beyond the 'spectacular' earthquake/famine/horror reporting of most TV news and current affairs.

Both Ann Zammit and Richard Bourne tackle the issue of the 'educational' forms of broadcasting which the Channel aims to develop – in conjunction with the International Broadcasting Trust (IBT). Here we return to the questions of 'feedback' and 'interaction' raised by Charlotte Barry.

CHAPTER 10

Channel Four and the black community
Amon Saba Saakana

There are inherent problems in the portrayal of black people in the British media, and on television in particular. The pre-war view of blacks as savages has not appreciably changed, and if anything has been reinforced in the post-war setting of a large influx of blacks to this country. The racism of the British is historically based rather than a recent manifestation, and this obviously has much to do with Britain's murderous history as a colonial empire. So the continued portrayal on television of blacks in racist and caricatured contexts is not surprising to black people. But when told that they are in fact racist, white people say that blacks have a chip on their shoulder.

I was recently buying from a white stall-holder in Portobello Road when she asked me if I had seen a recent TV programme on racist practices in employment. I told the otherwise jovial young lady I had not. She then said: 'What a lot of bollocks'. A white customer overheard the conversation and added: 'The way they put it over on the telly makes it look like only blacks suffer unemployment. I know that isn't true because my son can't get a job'. These sort of comments are frequently heard on the street, and are characteristic of the British attitude to the realities of racism.

A friend later told me that the producers of the programme in question had set up a black youth to be interviewed for a job – only to be told by the employer that the vacancy was filled. The producers then had a white girl phone up for the same job, and the employer stated that the job was still vacant. Yet this clear demonstration of racism in the programme was completely denied by the white stall-holder and her customer.

A racist psychology

This maddening attitude to the seen manifestations of racism by white people illustrates a particular mentality. Racism is not confined to the mere act of racist practice, but is fundamentally grounded in the psychological framework of the white British mind. What has made that mind so unbending, so oblivious to the facts of 20th century existence in Britain? Firstly, as Enoch Powell correctly defined the characteristics of a British person, it is an accumulation of traditional institutions. Secondly, those institutions were developed through class distinctions and separations: made more monstrous by the invention of racial superiority. Their savage destruction of ancient civilisations forced Europeans to characterise the Afrikan/ Asian as the colonised and exploited, and to project those characteristics as innate, as if to say that blacks were 'born like that'.

This is reflected in the way in which the black person is seen in the media, and on television in particular. The most common stereotypes are the criminal (*Wolcott*, for example), the bus conductor (most of television), the incoherent and farcical (*Gloo Joo*, the best example), the person most likely to be murdered in any combination of black and white (most of television); and if the black man is seen in a positive light he is usually patriotic and speaks with the best upper class British accent (*Department S*). There were and are no inbetweens. More recent attempts at comedy have seen the canonisation of a black coon, Lennie Henry, who caricatures Rastas (wearing an oversized red, gold and green tam) in an awful Jamaican accent and does exactly the same to Afrikans ('Katanga, katanga' his famous greeting), particularly from Zimbabwe. Of course the programme, *OTT*, (Over The Top), included Lennie Henry to demonstrate that television isn't racist – that a black man can be a successful comedian. But the question is, whose values established him to be successful and who is he funny to? Certainly not black people!

If that is how blacks are presently treated on television, what does the new channel hope to achieve? According to the mandate granted by the IBA, the fourth channel was set up to deal with areas of broadcasting not covered by existing television.

At the same time, it has always been a known fact (amongst TV producers) that the so-called ethnic minorities have never been happy with the way in which television has reflected their culture. This provided one of the principle reasons for Channel Four's emergence.

Yet in practice, the so-called ethnic minorities – or as I would prefer to term them, alternative cultures – have virtually no voice in the programming of Channel Four. There are 18 editorial posts on Channel Four, and with one exception, all are controlled by white people. This unmistakable bias in the selection of staff means that the only black person employed (and a person of visibly mixed, black/white parentage) is given the job of relating to blacks only! Thus at this executive level where a strong voice is desperately needed to fight for challenging black programme ideas, there is only one black voice. (Thus Channel Four's own expensive colour blurb promise that it 'has been charged by an Act of Parliament to provide a distinctive service' (i.e. distinctive from the rest of television), has already fallen into the rotten dung heap of mainstream television through both staffing decisions and the farming out of multi-million pound contracts to primarily white production companies.)

Processes of exclusion

Channel Four is funded by subscription paid by the ITV companies through the IBA. That will amount to £104 million by March 1983. In its first financial year of operation, since officially coming into existence in January 1981, something in the region of £100 million in contracts have already been signed. There is clearly a scarcity of black programme makers in this country, due to no fault of black people themselves, but due largely to the racism of television. 98 per cent of the major contracts have been granted by the new channel to white production companies.

Channel Four justifies this practice by saying there were no black people to whom to contract these programmes. Basil Davidson, for example, a man who has done a great deal to enlighten Europeans about black history, was given £500,000 to make a series of films about Afrikan history. But by selecting Davidson, a white man, Channel Four was telling black people that they had no significant historians. At a later meeting where this was discussed, the commissioning editor replied to my point about Cheik Anta-Diop[1] being an eminently more qualified person – he has a vast array of inter-disciplinary academic qualifications besides deep scholastic interest, and has been working in the area for the last 35 years – by saying that her approach was that no single black historian should be given the job of making such a programme. Yet Basil Davidson, a white man, was precisely a single white historian given the financial backing and a white crew to make a non-racist series about black people! She later confessed that it was not her decision to commission Basil Davidson and that she was hired subsequently.

One can also look at the way in which Channel Four has turned to the mainstream television orthodoxies in constructing a supposedly alternative perspective on the news. Instead of setting up an independent news production company, Channel Four has asked ITN to provide the daily news slot – because, it is claimed, ITN has the facilities. But if you are talking about alternative news presentation, does ITN have the personnel with the appropriate orientation to reflect a different perspective? It is like a pig being pregnant and dropping a cat! Another dagger in the heart of Channel Four's supposedly progressive policies appeared in Jeremy Isaacs' response to a question raised at the National Film Theatre. In his reply he refused to request from the white companies (who were getting the giant's share of Channel Four's contracts) that they exercise an equal opportunities policy in the hiring of staff.

Diverse Production is attempting to make a significant initiative in the area of Channel Four's news programming. This company is headed by an ex-*Panorama* producer, David Graham, who claims that the alternative news they have in mind is the presentation of views, whether in the minority or not, that are bypassed by mainstream television. The problem here is that mainstream television news already expresses racist, biased and middle-class views on any given subject, and Diverse Production might be said to be producing a complement rather than an alternative to the mainstream: they will end up giving precious air space to the National Front, Labour Left, Tory Right, trade unionists, management and so on – rather than taking a stand on these issues. Diverse intends to let the views expressed speak for themselves. Thus the meaning of *alternative* is being cleverly manipulated to the reproduction of the received and accepted. This certainly does not advance television news presentation in any meaningful way.

It is interesting to note at this point that two black journalists/programme makers, Imruh Caesar and Mike Phillips, did put in a bid to present a weekly current affairs programme, similar to *This Week*. They were in fact granted research funds, did an excellent job and finally presented a 60-page document on their findings. But the result was that instead of their diligence being rewarded immediately by a programme contract, Channel Four instead sent out the research material to existing white production companies, presumably to familiarise them with the black viewpoint, whilst Caesar and Phillips were told to hold on until the Summer of 1983. By funding the research project Channel Four therefore got an insight into the principles animating the black sensibility and relatively cheaply.

The extremely competitive spirit which surrounds the awarding of contracts at Channel Four also does not make it easy for the black programme maker to extract any meaningful prizes. David Putnam, for example, a highly successful white producer with major films to his credit, is pitted against Horace Ové, a highly creative and experienced television and film director, but black. Putnam is backed by the massive Pearson Longman Group with a £10 million investment, thus making the realisation of Channel Four contracts that much easier through co-production deals, whilst Ové's fledgling company, with a shoe-string budget may soon go under. Ové has experienced many problems with Channel Four's budgeting account-ants. He was comissioned to make a 50-minute film on an Indian com-poser/violinist who successfully fuses Indo-European music. This was budgeted at £40,000, but finally went over budget by £10,000. The response from Channel Four was livid. The Channel has generally under-budgeted its commissioned programmes, but one can only speculate on what happens when a feature film or series of document-aries being handled by a white film maker goes over budget.

In fact, out of the money spent by the Channel (nearly £100m up to March 1983), less than £1m has reached black-managed produc-tion companies. If a black writer submits an idea directly to Channel Four it is very likely to go nowhere. If, however, that same idea is submitted through a white production company, with 'credibility', it is much more likely to materialise as a programme. Thus whites are fronting blacks to get a foot in the door of a Channel that got its mandate through the promise of a 'distinctive' service – a distinc-tiveness that is increasingly difficult to perceive.

The appearance of Channel Four symbolises the development of a certain era. That era has already been foreshadowed by wide-spread violence, both in this country and in the USA on the part of black youths in response to their depressing and degrading social situation. Against that background, there is a necessity to create an *illusion* that blacks are succeeding in this country, and that illusion is best structured around the exploitation of the visual medium. In other words, show more blacks on TV, create a 'positive' image, and hopefully, young blacks will cease violent protest, and ignore their dire social situation. In a capitalist society, which Britain is, it is difficult, in fact, to conceive of the notion of fair reflection, that is proportional time/space for black people on television, or that those images might ever be controlled by black programme makers.

In July 1981 I was unhappily engaged as a researcher on a pro-gramme that the BBC's *Panorama* was making about black youths – in reaction, obviously to the violent uprising of that summer. The producer promised the world and used that dangerous word 'con-sulted' in our discussions – saying that I was to be consulted before the programme was aired. The end product did not reflect any of the ideas we worked on. The educational system was condemned by blacks, but this was cut out; a political group, the Pan-Afrikan Con-gress Movement which motivated young blacks to transcend their stifling social situation was left out; and the narration, which the producer promised would not reflect his opinions, but simply be used as a pointer to the visuals, was horribly racist. This was *con-sultation* in action!

Channel Four recognises that black programme makers are motivated by a compelling passion to control the images of black people reflected on television. But they are in fact merely creating the illusion that black people are being given access to television, while on the other hand controlling what finances they receive, what programmes they can make and who they are to work with. The continued operation of the buddy-buddy system is, of course, the modus operandi in television, and so Michael Hastings, whose past work is racist in this writer's view, wins a contract from Channel Four to do a documentary on Marcus Garvey. We have already seen what he has done with *Gloo Joo* and *Full Frontal* – that is, degrade the black individual and demonstrate his basic lack of understanding of the particularity of nation language (the differing modes of language emanating from island to island in the Caribbean). It is therefore more than likely that Hastings will get the white experts to justify his attacks on Marcus Garvey with scholastic sounding phrases.

That Channel Four's administration is bereft of any type of political philosophy which can place it in sympathy with the aspirations of black people can be seen by . . . contrasting it with the *active policies* of the Greater London Council. The GLC recently created a special fund for ethnic i.e. black grant applications, and has hired three black people to directly administer the fund. They in turn are advised by a black body. Furthermore they have increased their annual budget from £30,000 to £300,000 – a ten-fold leap. What has made the GLC change its policies as regards black people? Precisely the same thing, politics, that keeps Channel Four straddling the black tight rope – but a politics of a radical persuasion. We cannot expect those running Channel Four to institute a political practice at odds with their gripping middle class backgrounds, which are very similar to those of the Labour Party and the Social Democrats. The result is an illusion of progress fired by a practice of retardation.

CHAPTER 11

Fourth Channel, Third World

J. Ann Zammit

Television is said to have become people's 'window on the world'. The little research done in this field shows that most people gained their (limited) knowledge of the problems of poorer countries principally from television and newspapers.[1] Except for the top social category (AB), these sources heavily outweigh the radio, books and pamphlets. And television is substantially more important than newspapers as a source of information on developing countries and world development for all social categories except the highest – where television and newspapers ranked almost equal. But a moment's reflection reveals how unsatisfactory this 'window on the world' aphorism is. For it raises the immediate question about the range of vision available to viewers through this particular 'window'.

To begin with, programmes about the Third World, or which make reference to Britain's relationship with Third World Countries, are few and far between. Admittedly, it is impossible to be absolutely precise about the extent of TV coverage of developing countries and world development issues. This is because the BBC and ITV both categorise programmes under extremely broad headings such as Drama, Sport, Schools and Light Entertainment. Neither provides information on how much foreign coverage there is, let alone broad estimates of the amount and range of programmes on countries outside Europe and North America.

The only firm evidence to back up the impression that TV coverage of the Third World is extremely limited in fact derives from an independent monitoring exercise carried out in 1978-79 by a Broadcasting Group under the auspices of the Centre for World Development Education. Concerned with the influence of TV in shaping the attitudes of young people towards development, this group set out to assess the extent and quality of TV broadcasts on development issues and developing countries. They therefore concentrated their attention on schools broadcasting and children's programmes viewed or heard at home, as well as general television and radio programmes that might be watched by children.

The results indicated that in schools broadcasting as a whole only 5% of programmes were in some way concerned with developing countries, and only 1.5% with world development – that is with the social, economic and political issues affecting world-wide change and improvement, including the inter-relationship and interdependence of different countries. These figures provide, if anything, a generous estimate since they embrace all kinds of information and images, ranging from the purely anthropological or cultural to the zoological. On general TV broadcasting the monitoring group reported that their 'analysis suggested that the percentages would not be any higher than for schools broadcasting.'[2]

In 1982 and 1983 both BBC Radio and Television as well as ITV and Channel Four are promising new Third World programmes. The BBC plans series for schools programmes, Continuing Education and Open University. Whether these will be additional to existing coverage is not clear, but the programmes will not be scheduled at or near peak viewing time. The Channel Four initiative, in collaboration with the International Broadcasting Trust, is discussed below.

Setting up the IBT

The potential power of TV to inform and influence, combined with its glaring inadequacy in relation to the pressing issues of world development, has been both a cause for serious concern among organisations involved in Third World development – and yet a challenge at the same time. In the past, development and aid agencies, educational bodies, church groups, trades unions and race and immigration groups involved in development education have largely concentrated on the distribution of printed material, and on the briefing of key people in other organisations involved in education and solidarity work.

But the total number of people reached in this way was relatively small, and cuts in funding from the government's Overseas Development Administration threatened to reduce efforts even further. Some agencies, however, already aware of the limited impact of this somewhat traditional approach and seeking a more effective means, were galvanised into action by the opportunity presented by the government decision to establish a new fourth television channel.

Initially, an informal organisation called the Fourth Channel Development Education Group was established to campaign for a substantial amount of time on the channel to be given to development education. But the group was not content to act only as a pressure group, and wanted to seize the opportunity itself to become a provider of programmes.

This has resulted in the establishment of an educational trust – the International Broadcasting Trust – a consortium of over 60 non-profit making organisations including development agencies, race and immigration bodies, educational bodies, church groups and trades unions. IBT has also set up two production companies (one charitable and one non-charitable) to produce its own TV programmes, initially under contract for Channel Four.

The issue, however, is not simply one of supply or quantity. For to those, like the IBT, who see Third World development as a pressing and crucial issue needing firm and rapid resolution, it is the overall impression that counts. What follows is an attempt to give a fair, if schematic, description of the situation now.

Third World on TV: disaster prone?

Television tends to be interested in stories not the issue. Therefore most programmes and reports on the developing world are eye-catchers focussing on the drama of disasters – floods, famine, earthquakes and disturbances such as wars and coups. This is further accentuated by the news, which normally only refers to the Third World when there are catastrophes or political conflicts. This gives an extremely negative impression of developing countries and their populations.

The real drama affecting Third World countries is the drastic poverty and exploitation which forms the permanent economic and social context for the mass of the population, who are only occasionally affected, if at all, by the more newsworthy hurricanes.[3] But the many programmes which deal with the immediate effects of such disasters naturally concentrate on those most affected – the poor – helping to establish the overall impression that all Third World people are desperately poor. Those of us who have benefited from travel or study know this not to be the case. As in our own society, most underdeveloped countries do have wealthy, sometimes very wealthy, elites and often a sizeable middle class. This is not to argue of course that we should not be concerned most with the poor and oppressed, but that we should see their poverty in context.

However, media treatment, like many development policy documents, tends to make frequent reference to Third World *countries* or *nations* rather than particular social groups. This is an effective means of depoliticising issues, leaving aside crucial questions about the simultaneous existence of extreme poverty and substantial wealth, and the social, political and economic structures which explain that poverty.

When TV does turn its attention to underdevelopment within Third World countries, the way it deals with the issue leaves the viewer with the distinct impression that this is purely and simply the result of internal factors and predispositions – climate, religious or cultural traditions, supposed lack of physical resources, to mention just a few. Past economic and political relationships, both imperialist and neo-colonial, if referred to or recognised at all, are not considered to have had any detrimental impact nor any relationship to present day poverty. In fact what little broadcasting there is in Britain portraying interdependence between our society and Third World countries bears a strong Western bias. TV broadcasts are more likely to concentrate on issues considered crucial to Britain's *own* economic welfare, giving the impression that it is the Third World which is holding hostage the welfare of the Western industrialised nations.

Furthermore, all this provides the ideological basis for the supposedly sensible 'technical' solutions to Third World underdevelopment. The view that past Western involvement had no detrimental impact allows the blanket assumption that increased levels of aid and investment from the industrialised West, and more North-South trade, can be nothing but beneficial, putting an end to the underdevelopment. This overarching framework of assumptions makes it very difficult for initiatives like the Brandt Report (which questioned this analysis) to be dealt with adequately on television.

This view of 'the Third World problem' which underpins the perceptions and analyses of most programme makers, and particularly news reporters, reflects the ideological structures of our own society. Thus TV programmes are informed by the dominant model of so-called development theory, which still holds sway in most of academia and schools education. This model of the causes (ignorance, ill health) of Third World Poverty, and of the remedies (modernisation, increased aid) has been persistently challenged within development studies over the last decade.

There is not space here to discuss this in detail, but certain important points need to be made. First, the challenge to the orthodoxy from the 'political economy of development' theorists, though slowly gaining strength within the ivory towers, is still regarded with suspicion and associated with left wing politics. Nevertheless, it has on occasion been possible for TV to report and discuss Third World situations in a more politicised way, and consider openly more radical policy options than for our own country. This is possible largely because the countries in question are portrayed as distant from our own in both geographical and cultural terms.

Television treatments of Third World problems therefore sometimes *do* contain elements of a political economy approach – referring to questions of class and power, oppressive elites and repressive
governments, and to alternative strategies of development, sometimes involving drastic socio-political changes. But programmes
rarely make explicit the connections between the West and the Third
World in a way which highlights the ravages of the past imperial
connection or, more importantly, the detrimental ways in which the
present world economic system affects Third World countries – particularly the poor within those countries. If we take this one step
further, we can show clearly how our own Western economies are
intimately connected with those of the Third World, and further
show the lop-sided distribution of economic benefits both between
countries and within countries. This, of course, immediately reveals
the very real conflicts of interest between different social groups,
and begins to challenge the economic and political system in Britain.
Raising such matters on TV, even if only in connection with Third
World development, removes that comfortable certainty that 'it
couldn't happen here'.

A wider window

How, you will be asking by now, does this relate to the new Channel?
In what follows I shall try to show how the International Broadcast-
ing Trust hopes to use the space opened up by the establishment of
Channel Four to give a 'wider window on the world'.

IBT is particularly concerned to ensure that, at least with respect
to world development, Channel Four does not become a high-brow
ghetto purveying formally didactic programmes to the already well-
informed. Nor does IBT intend to concentrate on the Open University approach of 'individual distance learning'. Instead, the group
sees two dimensions to its educational work in relation to Channel
Four, and is developing a democratic structure which will facilitate
both.

First, efforts must be made to turn the area of common interest
which unites IBT member organisations – Britain and the Third
World – into a more generalised concern in this country. This means
screening lively programmes on a range of development issues
designed for the ordinary viewer – raising both the problems and
needs of Third World peoples and the conflicts of interest between
the more industrialised nations and underdeveloped countries.

In addition, however, these same programmes will serve as the
basis for a wide range of adult education activities to be coordinated

by the IBT network through its local committees. While IBT itself will make provision for voluntary adult education groups, it will also encourage other institutions to organise educational activities in relation to IBT's Channel Four programmes. The aim is to encourage the widest possible creative use of the individual programmes and mini-series both during and after they're screened. Home viewers of the live broadcast will be encouraged to consider joining some form of group educational activity but, for those who prefer, a home study guide will be provided.

The second major dimension to which IBT attaches considerable importance is an educational process in relation to the media itself. The fact that Channel Four will not be making its own programmes offers some scope for a more open and participatory media. It is up to the public to make this a reality by seeking ways to influence Channel Four to buy in the types of programmes they want to see. But this will not be enough. The IBT, for example, is not content just to establish a film-making capacity to provide programmes commissioned by Channel Four. It is also developing a democratic structure which will encourage as many people as possible to participate in the process, from generation of film ideas right through to final use.

It would be surprising if all was plain sailing, especially since there are many obvious tensions and problems surrounding the IBT project. Channel Four will expect first class programmes and cannot afford to make concessions because staff and supporters of the IBT member organisations participate in the elaboration of programme ideas. Furthermore, the IBT knows that its overall educational aims will be undermined if programmes fail to attract large audiences and a wide range of viewers. Good quality, attractive and non-studio basd instructional programmes are not cheap to make, especially when a substantial part have to be filmed in Third World countries. If Channel Four is to take its educational remit seriously it will need to provide realistic budgets.

Finally, Channel Four will need to accept that by giving more coverage to Third World issues in a way not done before – by looking more closely at our involvement in world development – sensitive areas of domestic and foreign policy will be opened up for discussion. The question is how widely and freely these discussions will be allowed to range.

CHAPTER 12

Politics of participation

Richard Bourne

Development education, still an object of doubt in some quarters as being more propagandist than educational, faces its most public test with the launch of Channel Four. Already 10,000 leaflets have gone out to adult education organisers and supporters of bodies like Oxfam and Christian Aid to tell them about the launch of a series of ten programmes, provisionally called The Politics of Development, starting January 18, next year.

The series will be the first offering from the International Broadcasting Trust, a consortium of over 60 charities trade unions and voluntary bodies such as the Workers' Educational Association. In the first week of Channel Four, in November, Jonathan Dimbleby will present a 'manifesto programme' for the trust, arguing that public and media attitudes have been far too narrow in the past, and hopefully generating interest in the series to follow.

In fact, just as BBC-2 and the Open University have pioneered a new combination of broadcasting and education which has had an influence far beyond its immediate target of second-chance adults, so Channel Four bids fair to open up new, informal learning opportunities for adults who are never going to be interested in degrees. Within this perspective, the IBT output has a special significance: it will show whether bodies which are not in the main educational can successfully generate an enterprise which is recognisably educational. It is bound to place as much of a strain on the voluntary agencies, now allied in 23 regional IBT committees, as it will on the programme makers.

At a weekend workshop at Nottingham earlier this month, laid on for regional representatives, some of these problems emerged clearly. National commitment by member bodies like Oxfam was not necessarily reflected right down the line. People who had joined local committees hoping for an access to programme-making were not necessarily as interested in local educational activity. IBT committees which had lost impetus over the last 18 months would have to be relaunched this autumn, precisely when they may be inundated with customers. London for instance, has yet to acquire this local support structure.

What is development

Nonetheless the IBT is already working at full blast from a small central office housed above the WEA national headquarters. James Farrant, formerly with Thames TV, is heading the programme side, aided by small task forces for each set of broadcasts made up of interested persons from the member organisations. He it was who felt that the outfit should start by making a series which would answer the question, 'What is this thing called development?'

He is therefore commissioning three sets of programmes. The first will look at development and individuals, comparing the effects of the capitalist free market economy of Kenya on specific people with the experience of particular Mozambicans, living in a controlled Socialist economy. The second will look at development and world politics, and will compare the pro-Western Government of Trinidad with the Leftist Government of Grenada. The third will turn Third World eyes on to the United Kingdom, and will ask whether social or geographical parts of this country are becoming 'underdeveloped' in a way that parallels feelings.in the rest of the world.

Academics and broadcasters

Whether this approach will meet the simpler opinion-forming, recruiting and fundraising goals held by some of the bodies in the IBT consortium remains to be seen. In the early days of the Open University there was considerable tension between the academics and the broadcasters, and the IBT is composed of bodies which are far from homogeneous.

The IBT has appointed Paul Gerhardt as its national education officer and he, helped by the regional committees, is trying to ensure a reasonable range of educational support throughout the country.

Mr Gerhardt is expecting the initial Jonathan Dimbleby programme to set off public interest. Twenty phone lines will be manned and a glossy publicity brochure, probably including a reading list and help for those studying on their own at home, will not only go out to every post-Dimbleby inquirer, but be widely distributed through libraries, churches and so on.

But there are some horrendous problems. Much of the educational world is used to planning its courses up to two years ahead.

To get much moving by next January, even in a member organisation like the WEA, will require considerable organisation.

For the local committees, set up originally as generalised support groups, there will be an inevitable flap in November to coordinate lists of events and courses and advise members of the public of where to join. Some things will be free, some will charge fees; in some areas there may be demand and no courses, in others there could be study events suddenly cancelled because there is too much competition for too few applicants.

Local study circles

As yet it is impossible to tell whether this IBT output via Channel Four, itself the product of a successful pressure group campaign, will be seen as a pioneerng piece of social action or just another resource. Although most of the country will see the first ten programmes at the attractive time of 6.30 pm it is quite likely that much of the more educational use will be on video. (A mini-series of three programmes will amount to scarcely 75 minutes, discounting advertisements).

On the other hand, some of the IBT members are rather good at papal improvisation, notably the churches. Among the church bodies involved are Anglicans, Baptists, United Reformed, and the Catholic Fund for Overseas Development, not to mention such umbrella organisations as Christian Aid and the British Council of Churches. Fully alerted, it is likely that they will be able to use the programmes in their local study circles at much shorter notice than a conventional educational establishment; some sixth form teachers could do the same.

The enterprise remains full of risks. Will the general public take to a dose of international relations on television wrapped up in the specific educational development and Third World guise which is being planned? Are the activists in the IBT member organisations, whatever they say about the desirability of development education, really willing to look again at their own prejudices and nostrums? Will they even want to watch television? Are they, in their own localities, prepared to do more than just congratulate themselves on setting up a media beachhead by plunging into some more participative activity.

Whether the IBT can really meet the hopes held for it depends on the practical answers to such questions and whether, at best, it could cope with the potential burdens of success. But the spirit of the time is in its favour. Starting out as a counter-offensive after the Thatcher

Government's cuts in overseas aid and the development education budget in 1979, the IBT has already seen the remarkable impact of the Brandt Report and the dramatic rupture with British parochialism that was the Falklands war.

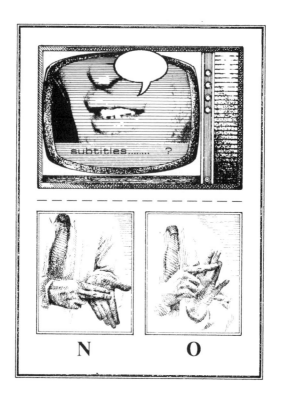

Forms of innovation and experiment

1. Organisational strength increases with time
2. Innovative capacity is inversely proportional to organisational strength
3. Organising for innovation is a contradiction in terms.
   – Murphy's Laws of Innovation and the Organisation

The Broadcasting Act 1981 puts a duty on the IBA to encourage innovation and experiment in the form and content of the programmes shown on Channel Four. This requirement has two aspects: what is meant by 'innovation and experiment', and how they are to be 'encouraged'.

The articles by Mandy Rose, John Ellis, Sue Clayton and Sylvia Harvey are concerned to explore the question of what 'innovative television' might look and sound like. We should remember here that these terms have no *necessarily* positive connotation: we could, for instance refer to Margaret Thatcher's innovative and experimental siege economy.

The search for new sounds and images has to be seen as one part of a much wider process, involving the development of new forms of work organisation, and new relations between producers and consumers in broadcasting. These new ways of working – collective production methods, for example – raise complex problems in relation to Trades Unionism. Undoubtedly the most interesting initiative here is the ACTT's recent Film Workshop Declaration (see *Film & TV Technician*, July 1982).

If one side of this equation involves trades unionism then, surely enough, the other side involves changes in technology. The Broadcasting Act does not deal with 'new technologies' (cable, satellite, video, infotec) – they are the province of separate, ad hoc, government committees. Both John Ellis and John Corner raises questions about the possibilities opened up by the changing relations between video, television and cinema.

Finally, the deciding factor will be how the Channel interprets its duty to *encourage* innovation. Will it see this duty as an unfortunate burden which has to be carried – by tolerating the odd bit of 'experimental/foreign' film or access programming – occasionally, late at night, rather than encouraged throughout the schedule? Or will innovative programming be separated off as just one more stereotyped genre – in the mode of, 'Oh yes, and here's another in our weekly series of boring/weird films'?

CHAPTER 13

Heard any good TV programmes lately?

Mandy Rose

Most analyses of film and television concentrate on the images. This article takes as its starting point *sound* and attempts to map out the uses of sound in TV and point to the role it *could* play within new forms of programme making.

Sound recordists and technicians often complain that nobody notices the sound unless it goes wrong. This is borne out both in the way that television studios and most film productions are organised and also in the way programmes and films are received. We talk about watching television, going to see a movie, despite the fact that film and television involve as much listening as looking.

A soundtrack generally comprises both verbal and non-verbal sounds. The verbal elements – dialogue, voice over, lyrics – are in a sense readily available for analysis; we can talk about what is said. But the non-verbal elements – sound effects, music, atmosphere tracks (background noise) – seem to evade discussion. On one level this is because they are deliberately employed in film and television as inconspicuous contributors to the meaning. On another level it is because, with the exception of music, they only make sense in combination with other elements of the soundtrack, or the images.

It's impossible to talk about television sound without reference to the history of film sound. This is partly because broadcast television involves a mixture of film, video and live material and therefore a mixture of recording practices. But it is also because the practices which construct the sounds we hear from our television speakers have developed from notions of sound/image relationships with their roots in early sound cinema. To see how we've arrived at current practices it's therefore useful to look back at the way sounds and pictures were first combined.

From pianos to Vivaldi

Though silent films were produced for 30 years before the first Talkie they were not in fact usually watched in silence, but with a piano accompaniment. The first piano accompaniment to a film was reported to have been at a Lumiere show in Paris as early as 1895.[1] Between that time and 1909, when the American Edison Corporation published 'Suggestions For Music' – a sheet distributed with a film to indicate the music considered appropriate for each scene – pianists would improvise their way through public film shows.

Our awkwardness today about watching silent films is not, as is sometimes suggested, that our experience of soundtracks has impaired our ability to enjoy and understand the images alone. For musical accompaniments were introduced to counter the ghostly effect which people experienced confronted by two dimensional, silent moving images. Music was added to match the visual vitality of the images with an aural vitality, 'to breathe into the picture some of the life that photography had taken away'.[2]

Music was chosen to be played with silent films on the basis that it should enhance the dominant mood of a scene, and books of film music were soon published under the titles of the emotions they might suitably suggest – love, hate, passion, melancholy etc. Overwhelmed with the demand for original material, the sheet music publishers (who in the case of Winkler/Berg also had a virtual monopoly on preparing the music cue sheets) turned to classical music, which was unprotected by copyright. 'Any piece using trombone prominently would infallibly announce the home coming of a drunk . . . Finales from famous overtures become gallops, "William Tell" and "Orpheus" the favourites. Delibes "Pizzicato Polka" made an excellent accompaniment to a sneaky night scene.'[3]

The relationship between music and image is often described as one where the image has a fixed meaning which the music illustrates. This last example of a polka enhancing the eerie aspect of a night scene points to the inadequacy of such an explanation. For the polka, a light carefree dance tune, is hardly an obvious choice. But here, with moments of silence added between the beats, its effect was apparently 'excellent'. The successful effect would therefore be to create a tension, disrupting the audience's expectations.

When music isn't tied by the words of a song to a specific story or set of feelings, we tend to resist the idea that it has meaning at all. But take a piece of music out of the context in which it's originally performed – the concert hall of Western classical music, the outdoor sessions where South African township music is played – and play it elsewhere, and along with the notes and arrangement are carried its geographical, class and political connotations.

In advertising, for example, classical music is used repeatedly to suggest reliability, durability, 'good' taste, enduring values: the use of Bach's 'Air on a G String' for the Hamlet Cigar advert or Vivaldi's 'Four Seasons' to promote Rowenta coffee machines, are both instances of this. The soundtrack, in this case music, is one of a number of elements, together with lighting, camera angle and editing, which work together to specify what the audience is intended to gather from a sequence of film or television.

Hearing and knowing

Think of a shot of Monument Valley; on the soundtrack, twangy country guitars and a tune being whistled by one man. The soundtrack informs us that this is not a travelogue of modern day America but a Western. The period: late nineteenth century: the lone whistler; the cowboy drifter. In this instance our familiarity with the aural elements through their repetition to the point of cliché in numerous Westerns makes us able to 'hear' and understand them without difficulty.

Certain television genres, comedy and advertisements particularly, play constantly on our recognition of the codes and conventions of the soundtrack for their success. An episode of *Whicker's World*, for example, which dealt with life in the Western States of America, would very likely use the music of the Western as a 'shorthand' for the myth of the Wild West, which the audience can be assumed to be familiar with.

Episodes of *Rawhide*, an American television series broadcast in Britain in the 1960s, have recently been repeated on London Weekend Television. They are interesting because, though seeming quite laboured to us now, they clarify how television style has developed in the last 20 years. That development can be seen, through the example of *Rawhide*, to have involved a tightening up of television's 'grammar' in response to the audiences' absorption of its form.

The theme song of *Rawhide* is sung by Frankie Lane, in a cowboy persona, which we associate through the opening shot with Gil Favor, the father figure of the trail gang. Opening with a shout to the other riders, the song is an exhortation to keep the herd moving at all costs, 'Keep rollin', rollin', rollin', though the streams are swollen . . . ', and a reminder of the 'true love', the mens' implied raison d'etre, 'waiting at the end of the ride'. The song is played at the opening and close of each episode over a sequence of cattle-herding, the dramatic centre of the series.

A theme song which contains such a bald statement of the programme's subject, point of view and morality would be unlikely now for anything but a comedy show – '*A Fine Romance*' for example, a situation comedy for which Judi Dench gives a deliberately flat rendition of the song of the same name. Documentaries are most unlikely to use a theme song; but they will usually have a signature tune which defines the programme's identity through the music's cultural and rhythmic meanings. For example, *Skin*, a documentary series produced at London Weekend Television has a signature tune which is a single piece of music played first in reggae and then in Indian classical style. In combination with the title sequence this music defines the programme's area of interest as the West Indian and Asian communities.

Within *Rawhide*, music which has no source in the narrative frequently accompanies the action. This is what is known as incidental music, of which, broadly speaking, there are two sorts: thematic and mood. Thematic music involves the establishment of a relationship between a musical theme and an element of the plot – a character, place or conflict – and the repetition or reworking of the theme. Mood music is a direct descendent of the piano accompaniments to silent films mentioned earlier. Sequences of chords and notes of varying rhythm and arrangement are played which work to determine and heighten atmosphere and tie discrete shots into a unified narrative.

Nowadays, because the conventions of the Western have changed, one tends to notice the incidental music in *Rawhide*. In an episode called 'The Hired Assassin', for instance, where the gang are trailed by a stranger, the ominous music which recurs with long shots of him watching the gang and becomes more dramatic on repeated close-ups of his hand hovering above his holster, is simply too much; we don't need all this information to understand that this man is a threat.

The major part of the soundtrack of *Rawhide* is synchronous (sync.) sound – that is, sound which is either recorded at the same time as the image or added afterwards and played back to give the impression that it emanates from the on-screen action. This practice is fundamental to both television and film production as it creates a sense of immediacy, a 'life-like' effect. But the apparent directness of sync. sound and image belies the complex process involved in achieving it.

Sound practice: smooth and neat

Recording sound for both film and television involves practices quite distinct from the recording of the image. On location, film sound will normally be recorded on to a portable tape recorder. In television studio work, both video recording and the small proportion which is broadcast live, the sound will be fed through a mixing desk, where other elements can be added, before it is transferred to the audio track of the video tape, or direct to the transmitter in the case of live broadcast.

Take the live transmission of a football match, for example. There will be a sound mixer at the football match ground who will combine the sound from a small number of microphones rigged around the pitch to cover the general sound of the crowd and the game. To this will be added special effects from a library of football crowd tapes and of course, the voice of the commentator. This sound will then be fed via a telephone line to the sound control room at the television company. At this point another sound mixer will add additional effects and possibly the voice of another commentator, or the presenter who is in the studio. This combination of sounds will then be broadcast with the pictures. So, even in the case of live television, what the audience hears as a continual unbroken flow of 'natural' sound has been constructed through a complex process of mixing and filtering various sources.

In television, the achievement of a smooth flow of sound and image, both within programmes and in the transitions between them, is considered paramount. What this 'flow' does, in effect, is to hide all traces of the production work – both the literal physical work and the process of decision-making behind it. And it is important to note that this desire to eradicate the evidence of the construction of the product has been the guiding factor in the development of film technology. In sound this has involved making accoustically controllable studios, camera blimps (intended to deaden their mechanical noise), booms (to get the microphone as near to the subject as possible without being in shot), directional microphones, sound mixing equipment and the crystal sync. system (which establishes the speed of the camera on the tape as a reference for synchronisation).

On drama productions and light entertainment shows, a 24-track audio machine will be used, which gives an opportunity to remix musical numbers, add sound effects and 'tidy up' the audience reaction. This last process involves erasing intrusive noises – rustling crisp packets or an untimely laugh – and quite possibly adding to feeble laughter or applause (although the IBA always deny that they allow this). To point to the use of canned laughter and try to outlaw it from television on the basis that it isn't 'true', is rather absurd, but very revealing.

Television brings together a large number of elements, ranging from the political position of the personnel through the technology employed to the combination of dialogue, music, lighting, camerawork and editing in order to produce complex and constantly flowing meanings.

Even in a relatively simple set up – a filmed location interview at the subject's home – a sound recordist is necessarily involved in making choices. S/he will try to ensure that the recording will feature the voice, in the sound perspective matching that of the camera, rather than the ticking clock, the traffic passing or the launderette next door. Though the microphone is a mechanical/electrical imitation of the ear, it lacks the 'focussing' element by which the brain filters what we hear, and so the recordist takes on this function, selecting from the available sounds those which s/he understands the director to require. The basic thinking behind dominant recording technique is to get a 'clean' track of the major sound source, generally speech or dialogue, and then to add additional sounds, background noise and spot effects, such as door slams, phone rings. This happens at the 'dub', where as many as 24 tracks will be mixed into one.

Hence in a filmed documentary about work in a factory, the recordist will do his/her best to get the machinery turned off for a shot of the subject supposedly talking as s/he works so as to get an audible track. Once the machinery is back on, the recordist will take a recording of that alone. At the dub, the background machinery noise will be mixed with the interview so that the words are clearly audible above it, regardless of the fact that in the factory the machinery noise could well be 'foreground' noise, forcing the workers to shout to make themselves heard.

In this case, a shot of the worker speaking against the machine noise to the point where the words became inaudible could reveal an aspect of that person's working conditions unlikely to be understood otherwise. In other words, the problematic or 'untidy' elements in a recording may have an importance which dominant film practice would deny.

The desire to produce on the soundtrack the aural environment which actually exists on location was the impetus behind the use of what is known as 'direct sound'. Direct sound, as the name implies, is sound recorded and reproduced with a minimum of shaping – often recorded on one omni-directional microphone and not edited or mixed with additional sounds in post-production. Direct sound is of interest as the major identifiable alternative to the classic sound practices so far described. However, there is a sense in which the use of direct sound represents a retreat from the possibilities of complex soundtracks opened up by technological developments. For a different approach it is useful to look to a few exceptional writings on film which address the role of sound.

Sounds different

In 1926, Eisenstein, Pudovkin and Alexandrov published a 'Statement on Sound Aesthetics' in which they called for non-sync sound as a principle of the sound film.[4] This view was based on the belief that the unity of sound and image effected by sync sound was essentially at odds with montage, the form of cinema they were committed to. Montage cinema is based on a dialectic between images, and was, they felt, best fitted to expressing the processes of revolutionary change.

Writing in the 1930s and 1940s Bela Balasz consistently pointed to the failure of the sound film to use sound creatively. His starting point was that while the silent film was a unique art form, sound had in most cases merely been added to film to adapt it into 'a speaking photographed theatre'. Balasz believed that, compared to sight, hearing is a relatively undeveloped sense and that the sound film has vast potential for the promotion of an 'auditive culture'.[5]

Composing for Films, co-written by Hans Eisler and Theodor Adorno in 1947, criticise the predominant use of music as an aid to instant comprehension in film.[6] The prescriptive sections of the book point instead to a use of music which could serve to distance the audience – engaging with the image more as a form of question and answer, negation and affirmation, than as a prop to enforce a single intended reading. Their approach has had effects on specific areas of film-making, most notably the work of Jean-Luc Godard, though TV tends to consign such innovations to highbrow drama slots.

But it is only recently within independent film-making that a practice has emerged which attempts a more flexible relationship between sound and image to create space for oppositional political meanings. Feminist film-makers in particular have consistently broken with forms of cinema which present the patriarchal world as unquestionable. In *News From Home*, for example, the Belgian film maker Chantal Akerman suggests the situation of a woman living in a foreign city, yet still involved with her family in Europe, through long static shots and sound effects of New York overlaid by her mother's voice: reading her own letters to her daughter. The dual soundtrack effectively emphasises a consciousness which is split between experience and memory.

The films of Jean Marie Straub and Danielle Huillet are of specific interest here in their central concern with sound, and their attempt to reverse the usual relationship between sound and image. Asked by West German TV to produce a short film which would visually illustrate a score by Arnold Schoenberg, Straub replied that music could not be illustrated optically at all. Instead they produced 'An Introduction to Arnold Schoenberg's Accompaniment to A Cinematographic Scene' which investigates the piece of music through the political and historical context of its production.

The bulk of the 15-minute film consists of a man in a TV studio reading a letter which Schoenberg wrote to the painter Kandinsky in 1922 expressing his anger at the anti-semitism of liberal intellectuals involved in the Bauhaus. About seven minutes into the film the music begins, accompanying the words of the letter. In this way the audience comes to the music in the process of thinking about the conditions of its composition rather than as the ahistorical expression of an inspired individual.

It has always been a possibility for commercially successful film-makers to make comparable major breaches with sound conventions. The soundtracks of Sergio Leone's Westerns, for example, especially when they feature Enrico Morricone's startlingly conspicuous scores, consistently disobey the rules of sound naturalism. By emphasising a particular aspect of a shot – say footsteps or the buzz of a fly – by unrealistically close-up sound, silence, contrasting it with sudden rushes of noise or pushing forward conversation taking place at the back of shot or out of frame – the aural elements are made overtly active.

Since the days when *Rawhide* was produced, the TV pioneers have ridden a well worn trail, refining but never really departing from it, as if a shift in style would necessarily alienate the audience rather than provide a welcome change. The nostalgia with which TV workers talk of the excitement of the early days of TV, especially 'live' broadcasts, illustrates the extent to which the programme formats have become matters of routine rather than occasions for experiment. In the sound department this means that technicians are employed to service productions with inflexible sound conventions, simply part of a production line which rolls out programmes. As a result, TV technicians tend to fetishise 'quality' (and the high technology they work with) as a response to their exclusion from the 'creative' side of programme making – seen as the business of the 'Director'.

It is ironic that now the facilities are available for combining multiple sound sources in post-production, these are used simply to reinforce prevailing expectations. This shift could, with a different impetus, provide sound workers with a more inventive role in the production process. With the involvement of independent film-makers in Channel Four, the space is now available to put together strategies developed outside the context of TV but with the technology available within it. This could mean some interesting listening on Channel Four, but we'll have to wait and hear.

CHAPTER 15

Cherchez la femme

Sue Clayton

In 1975, when I was studying photography, a journalist told me that if his paper were covering a story about a woman, he'd go for a full-length shot to get her legs in the picture. 'But – that's *sexist*!' I gasped. It at least had the charm of relative novelty in those days. 'No, it's not,' countered the hack jovially, 'if I'd just done her head and shoulders, you'd have said I only wanted to show a pretty face. And if I'd done anything *else*...' Cue for Big Laughs.

Describing anything as sexist in those early days was like lobbing a grenade in what you thought was more or less the enemy's direction. You heaved it into the air and hoped for a direct hit. Sometimes, as in the exchange above, it came back again, and attached to it were accusations of being impossible to please. This was especially true in debates around cinema: while it was easy to spot the sexist image, it wasn't so easy to imagine a ... what? Positive image? Perfect Feminist film?

Real Woman

In those days though, it was easy enough to identify the movie stereotypes – virgin, whore; namby-pamby, double-crosser; girls who Did, girls who Didn't. There was an assumption that Hollywood in particular showed a 'false' view of women and that the 'truth' was reality, ordinariness. So the new generation of feminist film maker began to produce the Real Woman.

Their early documentaries tended to minimise cinematic devices and concentrate on having women directly address their oppression to the camera. The effect was to make the person on the screen one of the audience, one of 'us', and to dispel the usual sense of alienation. The problem, of course, is that there is a limit to what the experience of one person can tell us, politically. And there is a danger that over time Ordinarywoman becomes Everywoman, brimming with sterotypical ordinariness and the imagery of laundromats and ironing boards.

Through the '70s, feminist film theories in particular were

responsible for taking up Louis Althusser's work on ideology and promoting the idea that cinema does not simply *reflect* reality, but in the way it presents images, stories and so on, actually *constructs* the choice of behaviour open to us. This was crucial work, because while at a tactical level we might remonstrate against Pretty Polly ads and the quivering blondes and brunettes of 'Dallas', at a more analytical level we began to understand why and how these representations werre so generally effective – what fears' and desires they played on. And from there, how they could be subverted.

But while feminists moved on, the cult of the Real Woman was destined for a certain success in commercial cinema. It was fascinating to watch how different national cinemas could latch on to the changing image of women and play it for all kinds of stakes.

For instance, British Television, for many years now the home of Britain's illustrious documentary tradition, and with a heritage of 'Up the Junction' and 'Cathy Come Home' could quite easily incorporate feminist realism into socialist realism.

In the cimema, films like *Family Life* could look critically at society through the consciousness of the female victim and at the same time reduce her to a cipher – worthy, virtuous and seemingly passive. In European art cinema, 'real women' were imbued with that old mopey existentialism (*Left Handed Woman*), the absence of starlets' make-up only enhancing the hag-ridden effect. Or, in American cinema where Real Women had a rather stormier time weathering such horrors as divorce, separation from their best friends etc (*An Unmarried Woman, The Turning Point*), the appalling self-sacrifice and unending moral courage that America has always expected was reasserted.

Strong Woman

After Ordinarywoman, Superwoman . . . As various alternative and oppositional lifestyles broke through into film and especially TV (single parent family, lesbianism, non-monogamy). I personally was torn between joy that such areas of our lives were no longer ghettoised, and dismay that audiences and critics were so quick (or by now so desperate?) to accept practically any female success-story as the stuff role-models are made of. Directors caught on too, and we began to see not the struggling victim but, tentatively, the heroine. Still when I look at films like *Julia* and *My Brilliant Career*, and especially when I look at how (male) critics have taken them up, I get a whiff of the patronising tone of girls' school stories: you too can be a role-model, warm, humane and courageous . . .

And aesthetically, feminists shouldn't feel compelled to like films *simply* because the heroine leaves her bloke/is 'independent'/ survives a crisis: besides, there's more to films than characters, which leads irrevocably to ... PSYCHOANALYSIS ... not a discipline to let you get away easily with talk about Strong Women, knowwhatImean ...

Mind over matter

The application of psychoanalysis and semiotics to cinema is impossible to summarise in so short a space (the debates can be followed in past issues of *Screen, Framework* and *Camera Obscura*) but its chief effects have been to make us think about the underlying structures of cinema; how film, through these structures, addresses certain fears and desires in an audience causing us to make particular indentifications. The question for us is whether women and men identify in the same way.

It's not only the plot which fixes and limits womens' significance in cinema; it's also to do with point-of-view and editing – the way, for instance, that the audience is shifted constantly between identifying with the protagonist and with the camera. Cinema is this respect is the ultimate power fantasy because you can 'be' the hero (hero looks, cut to woman looked-at) and simultaneously you can be a voyeur of all or any of the characters. All the danger of flying a plane and all the safety of an automatic pilot if a bit of turbulent contradiction comes along.

Watching cinema is a particularly classic act of voyeurism, and there is no doubt that male desire (and potential threats to the male unconscious such as the aggressive 'phallic' woman) can be played out, in rapturous narratives, with the audience's trembling ego safely concealed in the dark. Not just *Emanuelle* but most cinema is designed to 'make you (sic) feel good without feeling bad', if 'bad' means guilty or responsible for the consequences of your fantasy-involvement.

Where to next? In an article in *Framework* (no 10 Spring 1979) Laura Mulvey proposes 'the necessity of counter-cinema, of exposing the force of pleasure inherent in the cinematic experience insofar as it is organised around male erotic privilege, and built on an imbalance between male/female active/passive.'

In terms of feminist practices (or can we by now assume that people other than women have an interest in this particular battle?) there have been very broadly two lines of pursuit. One has been film making and criticism which attacks the existing system and continually points to the enforced silence of women's desire. The other sees the possibility of an autonomous women's culture, a space *within* patriarchal values. Which is what the following story is about.

Pleasure

I was one of a spiky-haired and dungareed British delegation to a rather steamy Women's Festival in Italy two years ago. We had been watching a film about witch-burning, which consisted almost entirely in a naked women dancing and gyrating for around twenty minutes. The exotic film makers, one of whom appeared to be wearing a lace tablecloth, smiled unconcernedly through our Protestant criticisms. 'We've been discussing this sort of thing for years in England,' I said earnestly. 'You can't use the naked female body anymore. It's always recuperated by the male gaze.' 'Who cares about men?' said Tablecloth. 'We make films for *women*. To *enjoy*,' she added darkly.

When you repeat this story, people go haha, yes, consult our desires, theory isn't enough, pleasure is the new term, etc; yet I've lost count of the number of times I've stood in front of deathly silent Woman-and-Film classes, rehearsing a refrain which goes 'What would you like to see films about? Do you have fantasies? Er-how about you over there?' Mildly scandalised response; should I have worn a dirty raincoat? 'Is there a possibility that feminists could produce say, a completely innovative style of heterosexual romance?' 'Ask a heterosexual,' says the woman I've been inadvertently staring at. 'I'd rather see a good cartoon with the kids' says another. Both remarks suggest a certain frustration with the current debate . . .

Interestingly, at the point where women's desire is on the feminist agenda, it's also in a very literalised form the Hollywood flavour-of-the-month (viz *Insatiable, Body Heat*). Which inevitably means that real advances in how we make and look at films will take a bit longer – because Hollywood's incessant conflation of desire and pleasures with copulation only confuses the issue.

Sacrifice and confession

Turning here to television – there has been a rather more curious hybrid of critical theory surrounding issues of gender. The problems are around the *viewing situation* of TV, which is seen to differ from that of cinema – no darkened auditorium, overwhelming screen and salacious stereo violins. So do systems of identification as outlined by psychoanalytic theory operate at the same intense level? The desire for certain endings; the peculiar moment between the last image and the house-lights going up; these are replaced in the world of TV by a continuing flow of programmes, viewed within an often busy and distracting domestic setting – hence the tendency towards cruder plots, easily recognisable stereotypes, easily followable voice-overs and documentaries, logos and icons, repetitions and serials and series to punctuate and make sense of the flow.

Within this scenario, TV criticism has tended to concentrate on message rather more than form or genre; looking through sociological specs at content balance, 'bias', representation of minorities and so on. It seems to have been assumed that the TV armchair guarantees a kind of critical-consumer status, safe from the rampant under-currents of the red plush cinema seat. Audience passivity in viewing is seen simply as a 'bad' consumer habit, like reading tabloids or eating junk food.

I would suggest that such criticism, in relation to the issue of gender, merely tiptoes around those areas of psychoanalysis which could broaden the debate. For the very sociology which leads TV criticism towards audience rather than text, stops short at examining the programme-makers' *Fantasy* of a female audience. Having spent several dozy days in America watching what appeared to be a continuous soap opera (with product-co-ordinated adverts – serial after cereal) I felt that the issue here was not the classic narrative one of 'Woman-representing-threat-but-finally-just-representing-woman', but to do with a definition of the feminine world in which suffering and confessional, endlessly complicated and repeated, are the key elements. Does the painful soap-opera world of confessing heroines and appalling self-sacrifice have a hold over one sex, or both?

In constructing a 'female' (day-time, domestic) category of TV programmes, how far are TV companies issuing a licence to import this emotional melodrama into peak viewing as a 'female' element? Feminists working in TV have occupied themselves mainly with documentary up to this point. In entering the field of drama, I would see the breaking of the 'family/adult' (read womens soap/ 'serious evening') programming convention as a high priority.

A whole lexicon, a whole iconography, has to be built up to deal with sexual difference as power-difference; its work to be done by everybody, and I sympathise with women who are getting tired of it always being designated as *their* issue (read 'their problem').

'*Everybody's* got psychology, stoopid,' says the aggrieved Miss

Adelaide in *Guys and Dolls*. But *especially* goils.' Enough of the especially. I'm prepared to be democratic about these things.

CHAPTER 16

New images for old? Channel Four and independent film

Sylvia Harvey

Channel Four, and the parliamentary debate and legislation that brought it into existence, have promised us a range of new images, new sounds, new voices on British television. We are also on the threshold of further national and international changes with the development of home video, cable and satellite television. Will the new channel, and the new system for producing and disseminating images and sounds give us something different, or more of the same?

We cannot answer this question, or organise in ways that will allow us to affect the answer that is given, without understanding something about the pressures and constraints to which broadcasting has always been subject. To a far greater extent than the managers of the film industry, the managers of broadcasting have always had to be extremely sensitive to shifts and changes in the political climate. So although the top level management of both the IBA and the BBC have always insisted upon their independence from the Government of the day, they have in practice responded to the real pressures of the gently conflicting political imperatives of successive Labour and Conservative Governments in the post-war era. The consensus of 'consensus broadcasting' is traceable to the correspondingly gentle electoral oscillations of this period, and to the general evacuation of any extremes of political argument from the political scene. This age of consensus in which political differences can be prudently accommodated or concealed is superbly summarised in a note from the diary of Lord Hill (then Chairman of the Governors of the BBC) describing a visit from the Prime Minister, Harold Wilson:

29 January 1969. Governors entertained Prime Minister to lunch. After lunch, when I invited Harold Wilson to speak, he asked that discussion should proceed by question and answer . . . On this occasion the PM did not recite old complaints. He said he wanted less politics on the air, not more.[1]

The national broadcasting institutions have responded to the various pressures from political parties (including the directive of 'less politics'), business and other interests through a complex network of internal self-censorship activated by informal and highly sensitive political antennae. The much publicised 'independence' of the broadcasting institutions has been the product of limited and under-developed forms of accountability, exercised informally as it were over the clinking of wine glasses at private lunches. Although it would be wrong to see the consensus of broadcasting as reducible simply to the consensus of those admitted to the magic circle of the dinner table, the apparently trivial phenomenon of private lunches does point to a general tendency in the relations of power in broadcasting, founded on patterns of informal accountability, directed towards a social elite of the politically and economically powerful. Little serious thought has been given to the problem of developing patterns of accountability towards the *majority* of the users of the service.

To make this criticism of existing methods is not to suggest that the democratisation of broadcasting could be easily arrived at — indeed, without genuine accountability in the political sphere, genuine accountability in broadcasting is unthinkable. The challenge that democracy — including the ideals of participation and accountability — makes to the established economic and political order is fundamental. Lord Hill's autobiography (written from the vantage point of 1974) is again illuminating and symptomatic of some of the deep-seated shifts and changes in the political arena that we, in 1982, inherit:

The last five years have brought vast changes in the mood of our country, even the awakening of a new kind of society. Gone are the days of a serene and settled mood and a wide area of consensus in our national life. Authority is challenged and not only by students. Unions are more militant. In the larger organisations there is a widespread demand from below for more and more participation in the making of decisions. The division between the generations is deeper and the division in attitudes towards religion, ethics, aesthetics and sex more apparent. There is public disenchantment with politics and politicians, with broadcasters being constantly blamed for the disenchantment.

A BBC which has to do its work in such a disturbed, uncertain and divided society, expressing its many moods and providing a platform for its many contenders, is on a 'hiding to nothing'... My trials, I suspect, have been small compared with those which await my successors.[2]

This sense of foreboding, of having moved down a road that may now be a dead end, derives from a perception of actual and impending changes and a sense that the balanced oscillations of the post-war consensus are at an end. The changes in consciousness and practice in the post-'68 era (the 'last five years') can be characterised negatively as a break-down of order and respect for traditional authority, or positively as the eruption of new and democratically motivated energies and enthusiasms. This new society, represented here in largely negative terms where 'consensus' is replaced by 'division', a 'settled mood' by 'disenchantment', has generated the debate about the need for new images and new sounds in British broadcasting in the '80s. It is this world of division and difference, uncertainty and disenchantment (in society and in broadcasting) that is about to be entered by those 'independent' film-makers previously excluded from the airwaves of the consensus.

The meaning of 'independence'

What is to be the role of 'independent film' in the context of the larger debate about democracy and accountability, the possible end of the era of consensus and the subsequent difficulties to be faced by broadcasting managers? 'Independent' is a treacherous and slippery term. The commercial sponsorship of television was introduced by its advocates in the 1950s as 'independent television'; conservative political theorists have argued that an MP must remain 'independent' of his/her constituents; artists have insisted upon their 'independence' from aesthetic and social norms. So what is 'independent film'? For Channel Four an 'independent' is negatively defined as any individual or company not a part of the existing ITV production companies; and in the interests of bringing new ideas and new voices into television space is being made for these independents. Some of these will be large, multi-national companies, but others will be small groups of film-makers without capital and with few resources. One such group of film-makers are the members of the Independent Film-makers' Association. A brief look at their history will indicate the ways in which their work might contribute to the development of more democratic models for systems of public communication. The principle focus of attention here will be on the ways in which some of these film-makers have sought to transform the existing relations of production (the actual practices by which film and television programmes are made), and the existing relations of 'consumption' (the ways in which audiences 'consume', 'read' or make use of programmes).

The IFA was founded in 1974, but its emergence can be related to two distinctive developments in English film culture during the

1960s. Firstly, its origins go back to the development of an aesthetic avant-garde in English film-making. This drew upon the art school tradition and the advocacy of modernism in the visual arts, learnt also from developments in experimental film-making in the United States, and culminated in the founding, in 1966, of the London Film-makers' Co-operative. The aesthetic and formal radicalism of these film-makers made them, almost inevitably, unacceptable to the mainstream film and television industries. Making their films very cheaply, often in their spare time, the film-makers were more interested in experiment and innovation than in reaching new or larger audiences. Many of these experimental film-makers were, however, committed to developing a new sort of relationship with their audience. They offered in their film fragments, elements, unfinished structures which could, as it were, only be 'finished' by the audience. Only the mental activity of the audience could make sense of these fragments, thus producing a final meaning from the film. Of course the audience had to understand in advance these new 'rules of the game'; without that understanding they were lost, bored or angry. And despite the elitism of this fine art tradition which communicated only with an already initiated minority, the new emphasis on the role and activity of the audience was a valuable development.

Secondly, the founding of the IFA can be traced to the emergence in the late 1960s and early 1970s of a number of film groups, operating as production collectives, whose goals were more socially, politically or community oriented, and who had particular audiences in mind. Thus, for example, Cinema Action (founded in 1968) made films for the labour movement; the London Women's Film Group (1972) made films for the women's movement; the Newsreel Collective (1974) made films for the anti-racist movement and for other campaigns. These groups deliberately rejected the dominant professional ethics of neutrality, impartiality and non-involvement and sought to work in a committed and co-operative relationship with those groups about whom they made their films.

New ways of working

These groups motivated by explicitly social concerns worked out of a commitment to the films being produced – often on borrowed money, donated labour or occasional state grant-aid; they were involved in production for primarily social and cultural, not commercial reasons. Unlike the type of the detached professional communicator, keeping the world to be investigated firmly at a distance, they were committed as cultural producers to investigating and meeting the cultural needs of audiences or 'consumers'. Isolated from the cultural mainstream, they were nonetheless part of and committed to a broader democratic movement in which the producers struggle both to take control of their own production, and to think through the implications and responsibilities of production through to the moment of consumption. In other words, they asked themselves the question 'Of what social use is what we produce?'

The struggle to take control of and responsibility for the production process itself has led some independent film-makers (including some who will be financed by Channel Four through the new ACTT non-profit distributing 'Workshop Declaration') to establish production groups organised in co-operative and non-hierarchical ways. This means that the traditional creative/technical distinction between workers is abolished in favour of creative contributions from all members of the group. Moreover, in asking 'of what social use is what we produce?' these film-makers have already begun to recast their relationships both with those who are the subjects of their films and with those who make up the audience. They have sought a closer more sympathetic and committed relationship with these subjects (and extended periods for research and development are a vital necessity here). They have not parachuted into a community in order then to exist at high speed, clutching the relevant 'ripped-off' images, or items of information. They have tried also, through the development of new methods of production and exhibition (including the screening of sections of the unfinished film prior to the completion of the product) to involve their audiences in a discussion, criticism and possibly reworking of the unfinished film.

There have been attempts also at creating systems for feedback, after the film in finished, so that the response of the audience can be fed into, and if necessary modify, the approach taken by the film-makers in their subsequent productions. These forms of direct feedback (discussion between film-makers and audience) developed in the independent film sector cannot be easily adapted to a system of television transmission. And yet the principles of participation and accountability are clearly also relevant there. There is an urgent need to develop imaginative ways of facilitating the creative involvement of audiences in the institutions that produce and disseminate public meanings. In order to achieve this, much more sophisticated forms of active feedback or 'audience research' must be developed; forms that go beyond the cataloguing of 'yes/no', 'for/against', 'on/off' responses; forms that investigate and respect the complex responses of the viewer, who is both a consumer and a producer of meanings.

The sound of new voices on Channel Four, the development of new production practices, and the desire for a qualitatively different relationship with the audience is to be welcomed. But these new images and sounds will only survive and be effective, if the producers succeed in recognising, and in serving, the cultural needs of all those previously silenced or excluded by mainstream broadcasting. Moreover, the successful production of these images is itself intimately bound up with the emergence of new social forms, with the development of new and genuinely democratic social practices which will not only need to transform the social relations of broadcasting, but also transform and democratise all the fundamental social relations and structures of our society. Only as there emerges an active majority, actively campaigning for greater democracy at work, for greater equality in the home, for more participation in social planning, in the publicly owned industries, in education and in policy making, only in relationship to these changes shall we begin to have new images and new sounds in broadcasting.

Re-thinking 'Public Service' TV: a note on 'New Images for Old'

John Corner

In its discussion of strategies for change, 'New Images for Old' raises in a preliminary way many important questions which will eventually need tight and particular answers. Sylvia Harvey's argument concerns the ways in which, in the sphere of television, the dominant market relationships of producer, product and consumer might be replaced by programming based on very differrent principles of funding, of 'the production role' and of accountability. Channel Four continues, in prospect, to be an opening for at least some of the kinds of scheduling, types of programme format and ways of addressing the audience in which any subsequent, more comprehensive initiative around public service communications would need to ground itself.

Commerce and 'need'

There are two facets of Sylvia's argument which requires more detailed attention. The first concerns the extent to which present developments in Channel Four have to be seen within the context of the shift towards privatisation affecting electronic media in general. The second concerns the adequacy of our presently abstract vocabulary of 'real needs', 'social uses', 'creative involvement' and 'accountability' to deal with the task of effectively identifying, translating into hard political argument and mobilising support for, the specific changes by which we believe democratisation could be brought about.

'Broadcasting' is clearly under notice of major change. The present experiments with Pay TV; the Hunt Committee's recommendations on the economics and policies by which Britain is to become a 'wired nation' through the laying of cable systems; the planned link-up of such systems with international satellite services – these are all obvious points of pressure.[1] Together with the necessarily slow push towards home video, they will significantly alter the way in which the important visual and verbal constituents of public consciousness and knowledge are distributed in Britain.

It would be premature to see these changes as representing a 'breakdown' of centralised broadcasting; or as initiating a de-regulation of TV/video which would necessarily be an enabler of 'access' and plurality in innovation. Recent debates about the lifting, at least temporarily, of the 'must carry' rule (the regulation which at present requires cable systems to carry all public channels in addition to their own offerings) indicate the way in which market imperatives and powerful interests are influencing the development of new technology. We already have some indications of attitude from prospective cable company executives – 'cable has nothing to do with public service'; 'Anyone will be allowed to run a channel. Mind you – we wouldn't let the weirdo's in'.[2]

Free enterprise?

New technology is revitalising 'free market' ideologies in communications, with their attendant 'philosophies' of consumer choice, demand-sensitivity, as well as their assumption that electronic 'audience-reaction' devices are the lynchpin of democratised television. The hard, bright conservative promise here needs to be borne in mind when planning for work in the new channel.

This then affects the terms and arguments through which – along with whatever alternative practices Channel Four workers are able to develop and demonstrate – the market version of 'people's television', its 'freedoms' and its future might be opposed by another set of possibilities. Here some pressing problems emerge: terms such as 'cultural needs' and 'social uses' which are commonly used in debates about broadcasting policy need to be spelt out in detail if they are to effectively counter the established standards (eg. high audience ratings) of what constitutes 'success' or 'failure'.

How will these 'needs' be identified? With what degree of agreement/acquiescence on the part of those 'in need'? What part might any notion of plurality play in the formulation of need-based policies? And through what mechanisms of representation, committee structure and public regulation might the relations of accountability be defined and realised and 'creative involvement' turned into actual people doing things?

These are the questions which those of us wanting to re-think public communications policy need to ask. Although there is growing concern about the media within the trade union movement, for one example, there is as yet no popular understanding of the policy and production opportunities which are potentially available. One of the primary requirements is for a great deal more politicised public education about public communications, rooted in tough arguments.

By lacking a degree of popular discussion and support which

alone can bring this about, our proposals are doomed either to drift into becoming anxious generalisations across some apparently unbridgeable division between 'real audience needs' and 'present audience satisfactions' or to suffer constant fragmentation as we try to catch up and modify the initiatives taken by private enterprise.

'New Images for Old' can, however, helpfully direct us to a strategic assessment of overall shifts in TV/video and to a more tightly-developed set of policies, taken 'closer to the ground' and designed for a push on public awareness.

The Channel Four Users' Group

Charles Landry

The Channel Four Group, set up in 1977, was composed mainly of independent producers who were concerned to develop the positive opportunities offered by the establishment of a new TV service. The pressure exerted by the Group played some part in ensuring that the requirements of innovation and experiment were built into the Broadcasting Act of 1980. However, their clearest success was in ensuring that a substantial proportion of the Channel's programme commissions would go to independent producers.

The very success of this strategy meant that many of those involved in the Group have begun to work for the Fourth Channel. To this extent it lost its initial momentum and rationale: its members were no longer on the outside, clamouring to be let in, but were already inside the doors, and were to that extent, faced with a different set of problems and priorities.

Early in 1982 it was decided to transform the Group, so that it no longer functioned primarily as a source of pressure on behalf of independents. That work is better done by the Independent Programme Producers Association (IPPA), the Trade Association operating on behalf of such producers.

It was felt that the Group should become a producer-consumer alliance. It should function as a forum for discussion and debate in which viewers/users of the Channel can find a voice, – alongside would-be producers – so as to represent their needs and interests.

The name of the organisation has been changed to the Channel Four Users' Group to reflect this new perspective (see below for Aims and Objectives). We see the function of the Users' Group as twofold. One the one hand, we shall be critical of the Channel at those points where it seems to us that it is failing to hold to and develop the progressive elements of its mandate. On the other hand, we shall be supportive whenever the Channel (as it surely will) comes under criticism which would encourage it to renege on those obligations. One obvious direction from which such criticism might come is from the perspective of a 'professionalism' which takes standard forms of programme-making as its touchstone, and criticises the Channel's experimentation for 'failing' to provide 'Good TV'.

The Users' Group will attempt to hold the Channel to the duties set out in the Broadcasting Act. It will counteract the pressures pushing the Channel towards 'safer', more 'mainstream', and more 'professional' broadcasting – in short, towards finally becoming ITV-2 rather than Channel Four.

This involves, for instance, campaigning to ensure that the Channel remains *open*: to new ideas, new types of programme-making, and to new producers. Clearly some programmes may be patchy, or rough – where they are, for instance, the first produc-tions of the people or groups concerned. But it is only by encourag-ing these forms of innovation, while accepting that not all experi-ments will be successful, that the Channel's development can be ensured. Professional wisdom tends to dictate narrow confines of operation. The Fourth Channel has been mandated to explore new possibilities beyond these limits – and will need to be supported in this project if ill-informed criticism is not to send everyone back inside the bunker of 'Good TV as we have known it.'

This 'Good TV' in fact only seems 'good' to *some* parts of the audience: there remain sections of the public who clearly find no attraction, or point of identification, in mainstream broadcasting at present. The Channel has, after all, been specifically required to cater to such previously excluded or alienated constituencies and must be held to that task.

This brings us to the questions of accountability and regulation. Here the argument aligns with that for a Freedom of Information Act: no genuine public debate over these issues can be conducted unless the Channel breaks with the traditionally closed and secretive practices of mainstream broadcasting – making information on its activities available regularly to interested bodies and researchers. In this respect the Channel should ensure that it makes itself one place where the principle of freedom of information is in fact practised.

As for regulation, it would be unrealistic to expect the IBA to take a lead on these issues.

For that reason we see the need for an Alternative Annual Report, produced independently, which will investigate and com-ment on the matters which decide the Channel's future direction.

The Users' Group will attempt, through publications and open meetings, to generate public debate about the Channel. It will encourage greater public participation in its operation, and will act as a forum in which the needs, desires and demands of viewers can be expressed. Better and more fully developed mechanisms of feed-back – from viewers/consumers to producers – must be built into the structure of the Channel to encourage a continuing process of audience response and involvement. Such forms of feedback can only be good both for broadcasters and their audiences.

If you wish to be kept in touch with the Channel Four Users' Group and its activities, please contact:
The Channel Four Users' Group,
9 Poland Street, London W1.

Channel Four Users' Group: Objectives and Aims

To provide a forum and information exchange for users of Channel Four, whether as independent producers, educational and cultural institutions, those seeking occasional access to the Channel or viewers; and to provide constructive criticism about and opportunities for public debate on the functioning and further development of the Channel. And in furtherance of this specifically:-

1. To ensure that programme output falls within the provision of the Broadcasting Act 1981, namely:
   a) that the programmes contain a suitable proportion of matter calculated to appeal to tastes and interests not generally catered for by ITV;
   b) that a suitable proportion of the programmes are of an educational nature;
   c) that innovation and experiment in the form and content of programmes is encouraged, and that Channel Four is generally given a distinctive character of its own;
   and monitor or commission monitoring of the output to this end.
2. To ensure that the Channel is adequately financed by the IBA to undertake its statutory obligations.
3. To publish information on the statutory obligations under which and the manner in which Channel Four operates that is understandable by independent producers and viewers, and provide some means of regular communication among them.
4. To organise regular public meetings to discuss issues about the Channel of current interest.
5. To produce where appropriate policy statements on Channel Four and related broadcasting and cable systems to safeguard the distinctive character of the Channel and to ensure its continuing development; and to keep under review the legislative and administrative structures of the Channel to ensure that it is as accountable as possible.
6. To seek public and private funds to pursue the above.

Channel Four Television Company Limited Terms of reference

1. Preliminary

The purpose of this Memorandum is to define and describe the activities to be performed by the Channel Four Television Company Limited ('the Company') as the subsidiary formed by the Authority for the purpose of Section 4(2) of the Broadcasting Act 1980 ('the 1980 Act').

This Memorandum has been adopted by a Resolution of the Authority passed on 5th December 1980 and noted by the Company by a Resolution of its Directors passed on 17th December 1980 and will remain in force until cancelled by and subject to any variations made by any subsequent Resolution of the Authority, notice of which is given to the Company.

2. Functions of the Company

The principal function of the Company shall be to acquire and supply to the Authority the programmes other than advertisements ('programmes') to be provided by the Authority on the Fourth Channel from the date fixed by the Authority for commencement of that service.

For this purpose the Company shall:-

i) arrange for the production and supply of programme items by programme producers (which may include, as appropriate, the Authority's programme contractors and Independent Television News Limited) and to the extent (if any) for the time being approved by the Authority produce programmes itself; in particular the Company shall itself produce all programme items and material required for continuity and for information as to other programmes to be broadcast on the Fourth Channel or on ITV; and for those purposes enter into such contracts as it may consider appropriate;

ii) prepare and submit programme schedules for approval by the Authority (in such detail and at such intervals as it may require) and for that purpose liaise and consult with the Authority and its programme contractors in relation to the programmes to be provided by the on ITV;

iii) engage such staff and professional and other services as it considers necessary provided that such senior staff as the Authority may from time to time determine and notify to the Company shall be persons for the time being approved by the Authority itself;

iv) acquire such offices, studios and other premises and such equipment and furniture as it needs;

v) liaise with the relevant programme contractors and with the appropriate officers of the Authority to enable the programme service broadcast by the Authority on the Fourth Channel to include advertisements supplied by programme contractors in accordance with the provisions of the relevant programme contracts;

vi) ensure that the programmes on the Fourth Channel provided to the Authority by the Company comply with the approved programme schedules;

accord with the broadcasting hours and times and technical requirements specified by the Authority from time to time; and that at all times such programmes comply with the duties and obligations of the Authority under the Independent Broadcasting Acts and the Broadcasting Act, and with codes and guidelines laid down by the Authority from time to time.

vii) consult with and report to the Authority on such of its activities as the Authority may from time to time specify.

3. Finance

The Authority will agree with the Company from time to time the provision of the funds (which will be related to amounts received in the form of subscriptions from television programme contractors) necessary to meet the Company's approved needs, and will agree arrangements to ensure the best use of money and resources available to both bodies. The Company shall conduct its financial affairs in accordance with such agreements and in a manner which reflects the Authority's statutory responsibilities, and shall

i) submit, for the Authority's approval, budgets for capital and revenue expenditure and cash flow projections at such times and in such detail as the Authority may request;

ii) have power to authorise expenditure within approved budgets in accordance with powers of delegation which shall be decided by the Company and notified to the Authority;

iii) not borrow or give any security or guarantees except within such limits and on such general terms as may from time to time be agreed with the Authority;

iv) agree with the Authority the general form of contracts and arrangements for inviting tenders and selecting contractors in areas of the Company's business where such arrangements would be appropriate;

v) supply such financial information as the Authority may require to enable the Authority to discharge its duties, including the provision of such information to the Home Secretary;

vi) agree with the Authority the form of its accounts and the arrangements for their publication;

vii) make use of the Authority's financial facilities upon such terms and to such extent as are agreed between the Authority and the Company as practicable and reasonable.

4. Remuneration

The arrangements for the remuneration, expenses, etc. of Directors of the Company shall be as fixed by the Authority from time to time. The remuneration and terms of service of such of the senior executives of the Company as shall be determined by the Authority shall be fixed by the Company with the prior approval of the Authority.

5. Policy

i)In planning its programmes and activities the Company shall conform with any statements of the Authority's policy on the Fourth Channel declared by Resolution of the authority or by any directive signed by the Chairman, Director General or Secretary of the Authority.

ii) There shall be consultation between the Authority and the Company

Youth Television is a pressure group campaigning for a more accurate and more interesting presentation of young people in the media, and for young people to have greater access to the media.

Ann Zammit is European Consultant to the International Broadcasting Trust, assisting with the IBT's educational work. She teaches Political Economy and writes on Development issues.

Notes

INTRODUCTION

1. See 'Local Radio in London', a report by Local Radio Workshop. Available from LRW, 12 Praed Mews, London W2, price £2.44 inc. p & p.

WHERE DO NEW CHANNELS COME FROM?

Part I

1. *Report of the Broadcasting Committee, 1949*, HMSO Cmnd. 8116, January 1951.
2. This is printed in the Committee's Report, pages 201-210.
3. See H.H. Wilson, *Pressure Group – The Campaign for Commercial Television*, Secker & Warburg, London 1961.
4. *Report of the Committee on Broadcasting, 1960*, HMSO Cmnd. 1753, June 1962.
5. As above, page 170. Most of these changes were never carried out. See *Broadcast*, September 22, 1980.
6. As above, page 246. For an interesting discussion by a Committee member of responses to the Report see Richard Hoggart, 'Difficulties of Democratic Debate – The Reception of the Pilkington Report on Broadcasting', in *Speaking to Each Other: About Society*, Penguin Books, Harmondsworth, 1973.
7. See S.E. Finer, *Anonymous Empire*, pp. 77-9, Pall Mall Press, 2nd Edition, London, 1966.
8. For the beginnings of BBC-2, see C. Booker, *The Neophiliacs*, pp. 242-3, Fontana Books, London, 1970, and R. Silvey, *Who's Listening?*, Chapter 12, George Allen & Unwin, London 1974.
9. A. Howard (ed), *The Crossman Diaries*, Magnum Paperback, London 1980.
10. *White Paper on Broadcasting*, paras. 17-19. HMSO Cmnd. 3169, December 1966.
11. Amongst others, 'Granadaland' was to be partitioned by the creation of a new Yorkshire franchise. Sidney Bernstein, the company's chairman, was reported at the time as saying: 'If the territory of Granada is interfered with in any way, we shall go to the United Nations'.
12. For details, see D. McKie, *TV File*, Panther Books, London 1968.
13. See M. Shulman, *The Least Worst TV In The World*, Barrie & Jenkins, London, 1973. See also William Phillips' history of the Levy in *Broadcast*, October 13, 1980.
14. *National Board for Prices and Incomes, Report no. 156: 'Costs and Revenues of Independent Television'*, para. 135, HMSO Cmnd. 4524, October 1970.
15. ITA, *'ITV-2': submission to the Minister of Posts and Telecommunications*, December 8 1971. See also the 'Report on the Consultation on ITV-2 held on November 2 1971', a memorandum prepared by the ITA of a meeting it called to 'encourage the sifting of ideas and the development of thoughts on what might be the best arrangements for a complementary and viable second ITV service' within ITV, just prior to sending the 'ITV-2' submission to Christopher Chataway. This is reprinted, as Appendix 6, in the *Second Report from the Select Committee on Nationalised Industries, Session 1971-72: Independent Broadcasting Authority (Formerly ITA), HMSO House of Commons Paper HCP 465, August 1 1972.*

16. See K. Kumar, 'Holding the Middle Ground', in J. Curran, M. Gurevitch, J. Woollacott, (eds), *Mass Communication and Society*, Edward Arnold, London, 1977.

17. Printed as Appendix 2 in the ACTT TV4 Report. See below, note 24.

18. For a list of (some) of the organisations and individuals involved see the December 14 Memorandum, page 2.

19. As above, page 5.

20. As above, page 1.

21. Reprinted in the SCNI. 2nd Report (see above note 16), page 329.

22. As above, page 331.

23. *TV4: A Report on Allocation of the Fourth Channel*, ACTT, London, November 1971

24. See *'An Alternative Service of Radio Broadcasting'*, HMSO Cmnd. 4636, March 1971.

25. The other members of the committee were: Peter Goldman, Hilde Himmelweit, Tom Jackson, Antony Jay, Marghanita Laski, Hilda Lawrence, A. Dewi Lewis, James Mackay, Sara Morrison, Dipak Nandy, John Parkes, John Pollock, Geoffrey Sims, Phillip Whitehead, Marcus Worsley.

26. *Report of the Committee on The Future of Broadcasting*, HMSO Cmnd. 6753, March 1977. See also the incidental comments on pages 155-6 of the Report.

27. As above, pages 229-241. All quotations attributed to the Committee are from this chapter.

28. See his paper 'The Relationship of Management with Creative Staff', printed in the separate volume of research, *Appendices E – I Research Papers Commissioned by the Committee*, HMSO Cmnd. 6753 – I, August 1977.

29. 'The National Television Foundation – a plan for the fourth channel', December 1974, reprinted in his *'The Shadow in the Cave'*, Quartet Books, London 1976.

30. Block, as opposed to the usual 'spot' advertising, bands adverts together at one or two particular times rather than across the whole schedule. See the Annan Report, pages 164-5.

31. See Annan's *'The Politics of a Broadcasting Enquiry'*, the 1981 Ulster Television Lecture given at The Queen's University of Belfast on May 29 1981, Ulster TV Ltd, Belfast, 1981.

32. See S. Fay and H. Young, *'The Day The £ Nearly Died'*, Sunday Times, London, June 1978.

33. See for instance The Standing Conference On Broadcasting's *Evidence*, page 35, London, January 1976.

34. The following summary is based on: *'The Annan Debate – A Conference For Practitioners'*, (transcript), British Film Institute, London, June 1977; 'The Annan Report: The Authority's Comments', in *Independent Broadcasting* July 1977, IBA, London, 1977; *'The Annan Report: an ITV View'*, Independent TV Companies Association, London, June 1977; ACTT Annual Report 1977-79; P. Seglow, *Trade Unionism in TV*, Saxon House, Farnborough, 1978; A. Smith, 'The OBA and the Fourth Channel Debate', in *Educational Broadcasting International*, December 1977; *10th Report, Select Committee on Nationalised Industries, 1977-78, IBA, Vol. 2*, HMSO House of Commons Paper 637-II, July 26 1978.

35. Having done badly in the Labour Party leadership contest in March 1976 to choose a successor to Harold Wilson, Roy Jenkins had left a job with the EEC Commission in Brussels. The contest was won by James Callaghan. Merlyn Rees, organiser of Callaghan's campaign in the Parliamentary Labour Party, became the new Home Secretary. See P. Kellner and C. Hitchens, *Callaghan – The Road to Number Ten*, Cassell & Co., London, 1976.

36. This section is based on Bruce Page's article, 'The secret constitution – An anatomy of the Cabinet Committee system', *New Statesman*, July 21, 1978. See also the retrospective comments of Lord Harris, House of Lords Hansard, July 24, 1980, cols. 601-4.

37. The Committee's proposed members were Merlyn Rees, David Owen, Joel Barnett, the Secretaries of State for Scotland and Wales, and Shirley Williams.
38. *Broadcasting*, HMSO Cmnd. 7294, July 1978.
39. For a discussion of these obligations see the Annan Report, pages 267-9.
40. See D. Campbell, 'Official Secrecy and British Libertarianism', in *The Socialist Register 1979*, (Merlin Press, London, 1979); J. Michael, *The Politics of Secrecy*, Chapter 11, 'Opening British Government', Penguin Books, Harmondsworth, 1982.
41. One opportunity was found: to steer through Parliament the short (3 section) IBA 1979 Act – Royal Assent April 4 – which gave the IBA the legal powers and finance to start the engineering work for the fourth service. But this was as compatible with an ITV-2 as with the OBA.
42. See H. Stephenson, *Mrs Thatcher's First Year*, Jill Norman, London, 1980.
43. ACTT Annual Report 1979-80, page 7
44. See the 'Position Paper For Fourth Channel Conference', by Roy Lockett, ACTT Deputy General Secretary, as above, pages 55-61.
45. *TV4 the case for independence*, Channel Four Group, London, September 1979.
46. For a short history of this sector and the IFA see S. Blanchard and S. Harvey, 'The Post-War Independent Cinema – Structure and Organisation', in J. Curran and V. Porter (eds) *A British Film History*, Weidenfeld and Nicolson, forthcoming.
47. *Channel 4 and Independence*, IFA, London, August 1979. All quotes are from this pamphlet.
48. Reprinted in *Broadcast*, September 10, 1979. Quotes attributed to Isaacs in this section are from this lecture.
49. See, for example, Phillip Whitehead's piece 'Jacob's Ladder', in *New Statesman*, July 21, 1978.
50. There are differing versionf of this remark. See above, note 48, page 16; *London Evening Standard*, August 31, 1979.
51. See *The Guardian*, September 15, 1979.
52. Reprinted in the IBA's *Annual Report & Accounts 1979-80*, IBA, London, 1980.
53. See Part II for a discussion of Channel Four scheduling.
54. *The Fourth TV Channel: A Reply To Proposals By The IBA*, (Channel Four Group, London, December 3, 1979).
55. *ITV-2: The Fourth Channel – A Memorandum from the ITV Companies to the IBA*, ITCA, October 1979.
56. A point made by, amongst others, Peter Lennon. See his piece on the ITCA/IBA memo in The Sunday Times January 6, 1980.
57. Bill 139, HMSO. The delay in publication seems to have been caused by disagreements in Cabinet (prompted by the Prime Minister) over the loss of public revenue involved in the launch of TV4, to which the P.M.'s attention was drawn 'according to Westminster sources', by the BBC's Chairperson Sir Michael Swann. See *Broadcast*, January 7, 1980, and *The Guardian*, January 12, 1980.
58. In this context 'programme contractors' are the ITV companies, *not* independent producers. Conversely, of course, the 'other persons' can be *anyone* apart from an ITV company.
59. See J.A.G. Griffith, *The Parliamentary Scrutiny of Government Bills*, Allen and Unwin, London, 1975.
60. The dates of the Hansard reports are as follows: *Commons* – February 18, then on March 11, 13, 18, 20, 25, and 27; April 1, 15, 17, 22 (am and pm), and 24 (in Standing Committee E); June 24. *Lords* – July 24; October 8; October 15; October 20; November 3; November 6. *Commons* – November 10.
61. Most notably for the Welsh Fourth Channel. See the article by J. Coe and myself in the *New Statesman*, January 16, 1981.

62. Commons *Hansard*, Standing Committee E, Broadcasting Bill, 3rd Sitting, March 18, 1980, cols 119-130.
63. Commons *Hansard*, February 18, 1980. As Julian Critchley put it: 'I feel sorry for the right hon. Gentleman because he is still foisted with the OBA. Even when the child was living, before the election, he showed it little or no affection. Indeed, there were those less charitable hon. Members who hinted at the time that the right hon. Gentleman was not the father of the OBA, but that the father, in fact, came from Derby. Not only was the previous Home Secretary lumbered with the OBA before the election; he now finds himself embracing the corpse of that unfortunate child and still having to make half-hearted speeches in favour . . . I think that we should stand for a moment in respect not simply for the OBA but for the former Home Secretary as well'. (cols 88-9).
64. As above, col 64.
65. As above, cols 51-2.
66. As above, cols 54-5.
67. Commons *Hansard*, Standing Committee E, Broadcasting Bill, 12th Sitting, April 24, 1980, cols 652-9.
68. 'Channel Four and Innovation – The Foundation' (IFA, London, February 1980). Reprinted in *Screen*, Vol. 21 No. 4.
69. For the background to this contest see D. and M. Kogan, *The Battle for the Labour Party*, Fontana Paperback, Glasgow, 1982.
70. Broadcasting Act 1980, Chapter 64. This Act was repealed, as were all the previous IBA Acts still in force, when the legislation was consolidated in 1981. This new statute, (Royal Assent October 30, 1981), is the Broadcasting Act 1981, Chapter 68, (available from HMSO). The Channel Four provisions taken over from the Act of 1980 now form Sections 10 to 13, 32 to 36, and 43. On consolidation see F. Bennion, *Statute Law*, Chapter 7, Oyez Publishing, London 1980.
71. Letter from J. Isaacs to the IFA, April 7, 1981. See also the subsequent Guidelines for Independent Film and for Independent Video, issued by Channel Four in December 1981 and April 1982. The 'British TV Today' paper is reprinted in *Screen*, as above, note 68.

Part II

72. In an interview with him in *TV World*, (November 1981) Paul Bonner said that the acquisition and conversion costs of Charlotte Street, together with the expenditure on equipment (including computerised business systems), and on the staff so far had totalled 'very nearly £6 million'.
73. J. Isaacs, Speech to RTS, Southampton, November 1, 1980.
74. For further details see the IBA's *Annual Report & Accounts 1980-81*, (IBA, London, 1981); *The Guardian* and *The Times* for December 29, 1980; *Labour Research*, 'Company File', April 1981, Vol 70 No. 4.
75. See *'The IBA's Financing of Fourth Channel TV Services'*, IBA, London, July 31, 1981; *The Stage & TV Today*, August 6, 1981; *Broadcast*, August 3, 1981.
76. This discussion is based on: G.J. Goodhardt, A.S.C. Ehrenburg, M.A. Collins, *The Television Audience*, Gower Publishing, Farnborough 1980; P. Barwise, 'So Who Would Watch a Fourth Channel?', *Broadcast*, June 27, 1977; Aske Research Studies in TV Viewing, especially – *Weekly Reach and Demographics*, March 1979 – *The Revenue Potential of Channel Four*, printed in ADMAP November 1979 – *Audience Behaviour: Predictable or Unexpected?*, March 1980 – *The Effort of Switching Channels*, April 1980 – *Channel Reach in 1980*, December 1980 – all prepared for the IBA, London; H. Henry, *The Commercial Implications of a Second (And Complementary) ITV Channel*, ADMAP Monograph, September 1979, London; N. McIntosh, 'Where Channel Four fits in – and how to measure it', *ADMAP*, February 1982.
77. In context, Channel Four – as a new national network – is much better of than the last one. When BBC-2 began transmission on UHF wavelengths the existing

sets were not adaptable (as they had been for the start of ITV). A new set was
required, and at the beginning of its 3rd year of operation only 13% of the TV
public could receive BBC-2. This figure had still not reached 50% at the start of
its 6th year.

78. For further details see: *Reception of Channel Four Services – The IBA's Plans.*
(IBA, London, June 9, 1982).

79. See Channel Four's company brochure, published at the 'launch presentation
and reception' for advertisers in the Barbican Arts Centre, February 1982.

80. The exceptions to this appear to be minority language and religious channels.
See P. Barwise, *Channel Four: Some Audience Projections*, (an appendix to the
Aske paper on *Weekly Reach and Demographics*, above Note 76); also his
Channel Reach discussion in *Channel Reach in 1980*, above, note 76.

81. See *Broadcast*, July 19, 1982, page 16. For a review of the £500 million plus
gardening market, its magazines, etc., see *Campaign*, August 6, 1982.

82. See *Stage & TV Today*, April 22, 1982; *Broadcast*, May 3, 1982, and July 26,
1982.

83. According to M.J. Waterson, (Director of Research, Advertising Association),
in his review of advertising trends, *ADMAP*, April 1982, pages 194-7. See also
The Economist's international Survey of advertising industry trends, November
14-20, 1981.

84. H. Lind, *Forecast of TV Revenue to 1985*, Channel Four TV, London, January,
1982.

85. See the interview with him in *The Stage and TV Today*, July 29, 1982.

86. See his letter in *ADMAP*, April 1982. For an example of the doubts about
Channel Four from the advertisers' side, see 'What Price TV Advertising?', *The
Bookseller*, May 29, 1982.

87. See Broadcast, May 31, 1982.

88. See the *Independent Productions – Standard Terms of Trade 1982*, (issued by
the Programme Acquisition Department, Channel Four). See also the transcript
of a Consultation at the IBA on *The Fourth Channel: Production Facilities*,
IBA, May 20, 1980.

89. Reprinted in the IBA's *Annual Report and Accounts 1980-81.*

90. Channel Four issued a draft schedule in February 1982, at the Barbican presentation. A later version was leaked to *Broadcast*, July 19, 1982. The Channel's
schedule up till Christmas is due to be published on September 14.

91. See J.M. Wober, *Interests Apart*, IBA Audience Research Report, October
1979; *Complementary Programming*, Aske Research, October 1979. On the
scheduling of BBC-2 and BBC-1, see P. Williams' feature in *Broadcast*, May 11,
1981.

REALISING A DREAM

1. J.G.A. Pocock, *The Limits and Divisions of British History*, Studies in Public
Policy Number 31, Centre for the Study of Public Policy, University of Strath-
clyde, Glasgow, 1979.

PROGRAMMING FOR EDUCATION

1. Anthony Wright, *Local Radio and Local Democracy: A Study in Political Education*, IBA Fellowship Report. Available (free) from the IBA Education Dept.

2. See J. Thompson (ed), *Adult Education for a Change*, Hutchinson.

ITN: MUTTON DRESSED AS LAMB?

1. See *City Limits*, April 2-8 1982, issue no. 26.

CHANNEL FOUR AND THE BLACK COMMUNITY

1. See his *African Civilisation: Myth or Reality*, Lawrence Hill, Boston Massachusetts, and *The Cultural Unity of Negro Africa*, 3rd World Press, Chicago, Illinois.

FOURTH CHANNEL, THIRD WORLD

1. Bowles T.S. *Survey of Attitudes towards Overseas Development*, Report submitted by the Schlackman Research Organisation to the Central Office of Information, London HMSO, 1978.
2. Centre for World Development Education *Where Did You Say?*, London 1980, Page 8. A report on Broadcasting in Britain – its coverage of developing countries and world development issues in 1978/79, particularly in programmes used by young people.
3. It is also perhaps worth noting that in programmes looking at the ravages of natural disasters the point is rarely made that in many cases the damage is so etensive because, unlike in more wealthy societies, investment has not yet ocurred in river canalisation, coastline protection, appropriate building techniques etc.

HEARD ANY GOOD TV PROGRAMMES LATELY?

1. There is no precise record of the first piano accompaniment to a silent film. But the evidence does show even the earliest films had some sort of accompaniment.
2. Hanns Eisler (with Theodor Adorno). *Composing For the Films*, London: Dennis Dobson, 1947, p.75.
3. 'The Origin of Film Music' by Max Winkler in *Film Music. From Violins to Video*, (ed) James L. Limbacher, Scarecrow Press, USA 1974.
4. Statement on Sound Aesthetics in Eisenstein's, *Film Form*, New York: Harcourt, Brace and World, 1949.
5. Bela Balasz, *Theory of the Film*, London: Dennis Dobson, 1952, pp 194-241.
6. See note 2 above.

TELEVISION, VIDEO, CINEMA

1. This definition of 'the Hollywood film' is developed, as are other points in this article, in my *Visible Fictions*, Routledge & Kegan Paul, 1982.
2. The best introduction to the various kinds of work, production and exhibition, carried out in British independent cinema, is probably *The New Social Function of Cinema – Catalogue: British Film Institute Productions '79/80* (BFI 1981). The Independent Film-makers' Association (79 Wardour Street, London W1) functions as the political forum and lobbying organisation for this sector of cinema.
3. The effects of the ideology of the family on taxation and benefits policies is explored in 'The Limits to Financial and Legal Independence' F. Bennett, R. Heys, R. Coward, *Politics and Power 1*, RKP 1980.

NEW IMAGES FOR OLD?

1. Lord Hill of Luton, *Behind the Screen: The Broadcasting Memoirs of Lord Hill*, Sidgwick and Jackson, 1974, p. 103.
2. Ibid. p. 271. This autobiography is especially significant in view of the particular history of the writer – appointed Chairman of the ITA (1963-67) by the Conservative Prime Minister Harold MacMillan, and Chairman of the BBC (1967-72) by the Labour Prime Minister Harold Wilson.

RETHINKING 'PUBLIC SERVICE' TV

1. See Nick Garnham's 'Sky's the Limit', *New Socialist* 5, May/June 1982, pp. 30-32 for a concise account of satellite and cable developments and the arguments for a European public service policy.
2. Quoted by Bob Woffinden in 'More Haste, Worse Programmes', *New Statesman*, July 30, 1982, pp. 10-11.

Comedia Publishing Group
9 Poland St, London W1

Comedia Publishing produces books on all aspects of the media including:
the press and publishing; TV, radio and film; and the impact of new
communications technology.

The Comedia publishing series is based on contemporary research of rele-
vance to media and communications studies courses, though it is also aimed
at general readers, activists and specialists in the field.

The series is exceptional because it spans the media from the mainstream
and commercial to the oppositional, radical and ephemeral.

No. 13. **MICROCHIPS WITH EVERYTHING – The consequences of
information technology**
Edited by Paul Sieghart
Information Technology is the result of the rapid advance of telecommunications and computing technologies. Books on the
subject so far have been confined to either specialists areas or the
needs of the computer buff; this book recognises that IT affects
every aspect of our lives – the political, social and cultural. Alan
Benjamin, Clive Jenkins, Mike Cooley, Patricia Hewitt and Stuart
Hood.
paperback £3.50 hardback £9.50
Published jointly with the Institute of Contemporary Arts

No. 12. **THE WORLD WIRED UP – Unscrambling the new
communications puzzle**
by Brian Murphy
Will the new computer-communications systems really create the
social revolution in work and leisure they promise? This book
attempts to puncture the hot air balloon on which the industry
currently rides by firstly cutting through the jargon to describe the
new systems – especially satellite broadcasting, cable television and
'informatics' – and then explaining how the world market is being
carved up by the multinationals. Brian Murphy's lucid text sorts
out the main players and their products and also examines the
options for control available to governments and citizens.
paperback £3.50 hardback £9.50

No. 11. **WHAT'S THIS CHANNEL FOUR? – An alternative report**
edited by Simon Blanchard and David Morley
Arguments about what sort of service a Fourth TV Channel should
provide go back more than 20 years. But now it has finally become
reality, alongside its Welsh counterpart. Will Channel 4 live up to
the expectations of innovation and experimentation – not simply
providing an ITV2? This handbook explains how a major new
broadcasting service was created, how it works from the inside,
analyses the arguments about what programmes it will produce and
shows how viewers can influence the content.
paperback £3.50 hardback £9.50